JUDITH

Martyred Missionary of Russia

A True Story

by

N. I. SALOFF-ASTAKHOFF

Revised Edition

ZONDERVAN PUBLISHING HOUSE
Grand Rapids, Michigan

TABLE OF CONTENTS

I. Happy Days of Childhood...... 9

II. Refugees 32

III. Seek and Ye Shall Find 43

IV. Persecuted for Christ's Sake..... 74

V. Dedicated to the Lord 123

VI. The Youthful Martyr 143

Author's Note 160

This edition of JUDITH is reproduced complete and unabridged from the third American edition published by Zondervan.

Copyright 1941 by
Zondervan Publishing House
Grand Rapids, Michigan

Printed in the United States of America

I

HAPPY DAYS OF CHILDHOOD

The Beloved Daughter—In the Country—Discourse of the Rabbis — Who was "Yeshua"?

THE LIFE in the home of Mr. Weinberg was happy and undisturbed for many years. He was a wealthy wholesale merchant of dry goods. Under his able management, the income had increased yearly. The business was growing and had been especially successful of late. But material welfare was not the main object in the life of Mr. and Mrs. Weinberg. Their greatest treasures were three lovely daughters who filled the hearts of their parents with joy and delight.

The ambition of the parents was to give their girls the best education and, what was even more important, to instill into them the good old Hebrew customs and principles of life, to plant into the hearts of their children the faith in the blessed Jehovah, Who in times past had greatly helped all true and faithful Israelites.

The family Weinberg had among their ancestors a good many fine, stalwart rabbis, who had jealously protected and guarded their fathers' religious tradition. Rightly this family was called the bearer of religious life of which there were only a few left among this nation, which is losing its religion more and more.

There were times when Mr. and Mrs. Weinberg were sad and sorrowful because God had not given them a son and heir who would continue their old family. The greatest grief in a Jewish family is the absence of a son, who has to pray after his father's death for the latter, to increase his happiness in the hereafter. However, such moments were rare, as their three lively girls always succeeded in scattering the clouds of sorrow. With their merry chatter, they filled the hearts and home of the parents with joy and happiness as little birds fill the air in spring with their chirping.

Judith, the oldest of the three, and the beloved pet of the family, was a special joy to her parents. She had developed her abilities early and proved to be more capable than the others. The early delight and interest of little Judith in religion and her many earnest questions about God, too earnest for her age, kindled the hope in the hearts of her father and mother that she would later become a "true bearer" of their religion and the traditions of their fathers. Often she would ply her parents with questions about the details of the ceremonial side of the religious life.

All old Hebrew customs were kept sacred and observed diligently in the home of the Weinbergs. The father usually told his eagerly listening daughters during the Passover celebration of the significance of the feast for the Jews. He related how in ancient times their forefathers had been slaves of a cruel, merciless tyrant — Pharaoh, the Egyptian king. He described very vividly how in a memorable night, the night of watching, the Jews, every family surrounded by their children, had eaten for the first time the Passover lamb with unleavened bread and bitter herbs. It all was done according to the commandment of the blessed Jehovah and under the direction of the

Happy Days of Childhood 11

most notable man of God, Moses. All was in readiness for the journey as the meal was eaten in haste. Their loins had to be girded, their staffs in their hands, and the bags on their shoulders. That very night the angel of death flew over Egypt, destroying all firstborn from the son of Pharaoh even to the son of the last slave. He told that God had commanded Israel after they had been freed from the Egyptian slavery, to celebrate the feast of the Passover every year on the fourteenth of Nisan throughout all generations as a memorial of this great and glorious event.

Having listened very intently, Judith suddenly interrupted her father: "Daddy, why did the angel kill the Egyptian children only? Were the Jewish children better than those of the Egyptians?"

"Yes, my child," replied Mr. Weinberg, somewhat confused by such a question. "The children of the Jews were better in the eyes of Jehovah than the Egyptian children. As a matter of fact, all Jews were better than the Egyptians. That's why God chose the Jews to be His people, that they might serve Him, the true God. All other nations, the Egyptians included, worshiped dead idols, which is hateful to God."

"What are idols, Papa?" continued curious little Judith, her inquisitive eyes fixed upon her father.

"It seems you want to know all things at once, my child," he said with a smile.

"Yes, Daddy, I want to know all, and you are going to tell us, aren't you? Please, Papa, dear. You are so good and do know everything."

"Yes, yes, Daddy you are good," the other two joined. "Tell us what are idols; we want to know."

"An idol, my children, is something men love more than God, which is being worshiped like God. But we are told by Jehovah through our blessed prophets to love the Lord God with all our heart and soul. The Egyptians had many idols. They worshiped the sun, the big bull-Apis, the crocodile. The river Nile was sacred to them, and they bowed before many other things."

"Papa, but if I love you and Mamma more than God, is that wrong, too?"

"O Judith, you ask so many queer questions that it is impossible to answer them all at once. Perhaps I shall do it another time. But now listen how God punished these Egyptian idolaters while He helped the Jews because they loved Him and prayed to Him only."

Mr. Weinberg continued to tell the Bible narrative about the departure of the Israelites from Egypt, illustrating it skilfully with various legends from the Talmud and national traditions. Listening attentively, Judith broke in with another question: "Father, why had the Jews to kill and eat the little lamb in that night? Why did they kill it? The little lambs are cute. Oh, how cruel are the people! I would never kill a lamb, and you wouldn't either, would you, Daddy?"

"My dear Judith," replied Mr. Weinberg laughingly; "in one evening you want to become like your grandfather, a wise rabbi. It is impossible to learn all at once."

"Why, yes, I want to know all, and especially why the Jews had to kill a lamb at that time."

"All right, I am going to send you and your mother again to your grandfather in the country this coming summer. There you may ask him all the questions you want to about your lamb and anything else that inter-

Happy Days of Childhood

ests you. He knows all and can explain everything to you."

At this promise of their father, the faces of all three girls shone with joy. "To Grandpa, to Grandpa!" they shouted in merriment.

Nearly every year they had been with their mother at the grandfather's home, sometimes for months at a time. Judith remembered well how frequently several other rabbis, older than her grandfather, but just as wise and dignified as he, had come to visit. She had noticed that they were in conferences whole days, sometimes even whole nights. She had heard them argue, sometimes very loudly. Often names like "Moses" and "Yeshua" (Jesus) had been mentioned. In connection with the latter name, strange words had been uttered — "deceiver, impostor" — and other similar expressions. She had been greatly interested to know about whom they were talking, but she had always been afraid to ask her grandfather about it. Judith was especially eager to know who this "Yeshua," the "deceiver," was. But now it would be different. Since her father had given her permission, she would ask him about everything.

So the happy life continued in the home of David Weinberg. Summer came and the girls' school was closed. Summer vacation began, and the family could now leave the dusty cities for the fresh air and beauty of the country.

Shortly after the close of school there was a great commotion in the home of the Weinbergs. Near the front door was the spacious family carriage drawn by two beautiful horses. It was half-filled with boxes, suitcases, and valises of various kinds and sizes. The

D. Edmond Hiebert
Collection

driver, accustomed to frequent traveling, was piling up the things so as to leave room for his passengers. Merry laughter rang through the house as the children ran up and down the stairs. One had forgotten where she had put her pet doll. Another did not know what had happened to the package that contained the presents for Grandfather and Grandmother. Everything was topsy-turvy in the rooms. The mother did not know what to do first. The girls were eager to assist her and the maid in packing the things required for the summer. In their eagerness to help, they hindered one another as well as their mother and the servant. Somehow the shoes that had just been polished found their way into the suitcase with the best clothes. Mrs. Weinberg's good new hat had disappeared and was found in the bag, after half an hour's search, with the things they needed for the trip.

Finally Mrs. Weinberg found herself with her daughters in the carriage, tired and worn out. Mr. Weinberg did not go. Business demanded his presence in the city. With a good-bye to his wife and children, he gave the last orders to the driver, and they were off.

The beautiful two story-house, located in the midst of the forest, seemed to be transformed today. Its owner was the timber merchant, Mr. Weinberg, an honorable rabbi. Though advanced in years, he was still very active and able to take care of his business. For several years he had been living alone with his wife in the quietness of the woods. His two sons were both married and had their own families. They also had been successful in business and had made their homes in a distant city.

Usually an undisturbed quiet reigned in the home. At times Mr. Weinberg worked for whole days behind shut doors in his office, or in his study with the Bible and the Talmud before him. But today lively footsteps were heard throughout the house, and the silvery laughter of delighted children filled the rooms. The three granddaughters had arrived with their mother from the city. Eagerly they unpacked the gifts they had been preparing with joyful anticipation for their beloved Grandpa and Grandma. In presenting them, each was eager to make the value of her gifts known to her grandparents, and in praising her own gifts created much laughter. They recounted all the latest news from the city and especially items of their life and success in school.

A happy time commenced for the children with no lessons to prepare. Whole days were spent in rambling through meadows and woods gathering quantities of beautiful flowers that carpeted the ground with many colors. Together with the older folk, they revelled in the beauty of the wood-life.

Shortly after the arrival of the jolly little guests, there came two rabbis, old friends of Mr. Weinberg from a neighboring city, to see him. The whole day they were engaged in a religious discourse. The women and children were meanwhile occupied with their own interests. Only Judith was not interested in the usual things today. She had slipped away from her sisters and returned to the house. She tried hard to be near the rabbis, and she listened attentively to every word she could catch. Mr. Weinberg noticed his inquisitive grandchild and suggested she would better go and play with her sisters, as the conversation of old rabbis could be of no interest to a child.

Judith was far from being pleased. She would much rather have listened to the discussions of the rabbis than to the singing of the birds just now, but she did not have the courage to say anything in the presence of the visitors, so she left the room quietly. But from what she had been able to hear, she gathered that they were arguing about God, the law, and a certain "Yeshua." She determined to ask her grandfather about these things as soon as the visitors departed. Recalling her conversation with her father at the last Passover, she was glad he had granted permission to ask her grandfather as many questions as she pleased. Now the opportunity had come!

Following a short walk after supper, Judith retired with her sisters to their common bedroom. It was a warm night. The sweet fragrance of flowers came through the open windows and filled the room. The two younger sisters soon fell asleep, exhausted from tramping in the woods. But Judith could not sleep. Her mind was very active. Thoughts about God, and the conversation of her grandfather with the rabbis kept her awake for many hours. Even now the sound of voices came to her through the open window. She could distinguish her grandfather's voice, raised at times to an angry shout. The others, too, sounded excited and angry.

Lying in bed, it was impossible to distinguish what they were speaking about. Her interest was aroused more and more. What were they arguing about? Judith knew she had no business to listen and that it was not quite right for her to do so, but curiosity finally won the victory. Rising from her bed, she went to the open window. Just below her were the open windows of the study and Judith could now understand every word.

From the first moment she listened she knew that they were talking about "Yeshua," whose name was mentioned quite frequently by her grandfather. Now, she heard one of the other rabbis say that "Yeshua" WAS INDEED THE MESSIAH of Israel Whom the Jews had not recognized and Whom they had rejected. Her grandfather and the other rabbi were eager to prove that he had been just a clever impostor and deceiver. The one side as well as the other referred to the prophecies of Moses and the other Jewish prophets. At times their arguments became very heated. Judith soon found out that her grandfather and the rabbi who agreed with him, not knowing what to answer, commenced to argue and to shout, while their opponent called them to calmness and sound reasoning. He urged them to search the Scriptures most seriously and without prejudice.

"Perhaps one day we shall have to realize and confess the fatal mistake of our fathers, and then repenting we shall have to accept 'Yeshua' as the promised Messiah Who has come but Who through ignorance has been rejected and despised," he said.

Nearly the whole night Judith sat on the window-sill absorbed in listening to the discussion. Following the debate, she concluded that a terrible mistake had been made sometime somewhere by the Jews, the result of which was felt even today. But only the rabbis knew, and they talked of it only among themselves, for some reason unwilling that the secret should be made known to others. From what she heard, she understood that the Jewish people had rejected their Messiah.

At the same time, Judith received an unexpected answer to a question that had interested her greatly and that she had asked her father — why the Jews in that memorable night of their flight from Egypt had to kill the innocent lamb. She heard the rabbi who argued against her grandfather prove to him and the other opponent that the lamb that was killed that night in Egypt (as well as all the other lambs offered subsequently at the Jewish sacrifices) were only types, prophetic symbols of "Yeshua," of Whom the prophet Isaiah spoke in the fifty-third chapter of his Book. The lamb being the substitute for the Jews died at the time when the angel of death smote all the first-born of the Egyptians. In a similar way to the lamb, "Yeshua" had to die for the Jewish people that they might not perish together with all others for their transgressions.

Judith heard her grandfather question: "If that be so, what then is our duty? What should we do now?"

"The future will teach that," was the reply. "But first of all we must be honest, and it is our duty to study and search the Scriptures more thoroughly and without prejudice. I am sure it will teach us all what to do in this matter. This is a most serious and important question for our nation and needs deep and earnest consideration."

As the eastern sky became tinted with red and gold, the sweet trill of the nightingale came from the bushes near the house. The air became cooler. Judith was still sitting at the open window listening to the discussion with rapt attention. Her youngest sister awoke and asked, "Why don't you sleep, Judith?"

Taken unaware, confused, and fearing to tell the truth, she said, "Listen, Ruth, how sweetly the nightingale is singing."

"Sleep is sweeter to me now than the songs of nightingales," was Ruth's laughing reply as she pulled the blanket closer.

"You are right, my sleepy little sister," returned Judith, walking over to her bed.

Being tired after the sleepless night and benumbed with the cold, she soon fell into a restless slumber. In her sleep she continued to hear the men argue about "Yeshua." Her heart ached with pain at the thought that the Jews had been so cruel and had killed Him, the meek and innocent Lamb; that they had slain Him Who had come to bring happiness to Israel. She commenced to defend "Yeshua" in her dream, and she entreated her grandfather, father, and mother, the sisters and other Jews, to acknowledge and accept "Yeshua" as their Messiah. It seemed to her that she must be able to persuade them all. But suddenly her grandfather, with angry eyes, harshly rebuked her. Shouting at the top of his voice, he said, "Apostate! Heretic! You have deserted the faith of your fathers. Such as you should be stoned!"

Poor Judith was so frightened by these awful words that she turned quickly and tried to flee from her enraged grandfather. Making a quick movement, she awoke. Opening her eyes, she saw her mother near the bed, anxiously bent over her.

"What's the matter with you? Did you have a bad dream? With whom did you fight? You talked so much and were so excited! It was very hard to look at you."

"O Mamma, dear, I saw many, many people around me, and I was so anxious to tell them that they should love God more and that they should obey the prophets through whom He speaks."

"What queer dreams to disturb my child. Leave that to Grandpa and to our other wise rabbis. Let them think about God, and you and I had better think of something else."

"But why, Mother, should this question be considered by the rabbis only? Why should others not be interested in it, too?" asked Judith, looking up inquiringly.

"Oh, yes, my precious girl. Of course anyone may think and speak about God. But in order to know anything about Him, one must study thoroughly the Torah and the Prophets. Without this it is impossible to reason or judge rightly about Him. Your grandfather and the other rabbis know the Torah and the Prophets well."

"Mother, do you think it is possible to study the Torah and at the same time fail to know God and disobey Him?"

"Well, Judith. What a strange girl you are. Who ever put such thoughts into your mind? Let's leave this for another time and now get up quickly. It is nearly dinner time. Breakfast was over long ago, and it's a lovely day. I sent Ruth to call you for breakfast, but she said you had not slept at night as you were sitting and listening to the nightingales. She suggested letting you sleep a little longer."

"It is true. I did not sleep much last night," Judith answered blushing.

"But I have had enough sleep now and will be ready in a few minutes."

Happy Days of Childhood

With these words, she threw her arms around her mother's neck and covered her face with kisses.

It was a most happy day. Everybody, even Grandfather and Grandmother, took a long walk in the afternoon. The visiting rabbis had left for the station early in the morning. Noticing how tired her grandfather was and knowing that he had had no sleep the previous night, Judith decided not to worry him with her questions but to wait for a more convenient time. She had many questions in her heart to ask him. Most of all, she wanted to know WHEN and WHERE "Yeshua" lived, what his life had been, and how he died. These questions seemed to burn within her more than any others.

A few uneventful days passed. One warm evening the family gathered as usual on the porch after supper. Songs of nightingales filled the air. The children were playing while the women talked. Mr. Weinberg was sitting in a large, comfortable wicker-chair, his eyes contemplatively fixed on the last rays of the setting sun. Judith decided this was her opportunity for a talk.

"Why are you looking so thoughtfully toward the sky, Grandpa?" she inquired. "Are you thinking about heaven?"

"Yes, my child, I was thinking about heaven this very moment."

"Grandpa, dear, please tell me something about heaven and God. Father and Mother have told us that you have read so much and know so many things. I want to know about God, too. Papa said I might ask you everything I wanted to know. May I, Grandpa?"

"I have read and studied much in my life, and shall be glad to answer your questions. What do you want me to tell you? What questions trouble you most?"

"Oh, there is much I would like to know. May I start right away?"

"Well, well, more philosophic questions about God," interrupted Judith's mother teasingly. "She has bothered us often with them. If she were a boy she would become the wisest rabbi who ever lived."

"Please, Mama, dear! I am not asking you now. I want to be Grandfather's most diligent pupil, and I promise to listen carefully to everything he says."

She pushed her chair close to his. Putting her folded hands on his knees, she looked up into his face and said, "The preliminaries are finished. Now the questions begin."

"You'd better hurry, or your preliminaries will last until it is bed-time for me," was the kindly reply.

"Well, then, first of all: WHO was 'Yeshua'? What kind of a man was He? Where was He, and what has happened to Him?"

The face of the old rabbi became very sober and grave. Looking sternly at his grandchild, he said to her mother, "You are right. Judith is occupied with far too serious questions."

"Why is this a serious and difficult question, Grandpa? I thought everything was very easy for you. Our Daddy said, too, that you knew everything."

"You know, dear child, this question in itself is not a difficult one for me, but the knowledge of certain things is not good for everybody. However, if you are very anxious to know I think I shall tell you. Nearly two thousand years ago our fathers lived in Palestine, that precious land which God Himself gave to them. At that time they were not scattered all over the globe as they are today."

Happy Days of Childhood

"Why, isn't Russia our country?" interrupted Judith, puzzled.

"No, my child. Russia is not our country. This is a country of idolaters, *Goyim*, heathen. Our rightful country is Palestine, given to us by God. There our fathers lived, and our glorious kings and prophets. During the last time of its existence our land was under the rule of *Goyim*, the Romans, who were very mighty at that time. These Romans were extremely cruel and unjust toward our forefathers. They were very much displeased that we worshiped the true, living God, Who created heaven and earth, instead of bowing before their dead idols. It was a most trying time for the Jews, for the Romans were much stronger. But Jehovah has given to His people the wonderful promise that in His time He will send His anointed One, the Messiah, Who shall free Israel from all her oppressors and Who shall reign together with His people over the whole earth.

"This glorious hope always has lived and still lives in the hearts of all true sons of Israel. All our beloved prophets, beginning from Moses, have spoken about it. Shortly before our forefathers were scattered there appeared a Jew, the son of a poor carpenter of Nazareth, who claimed to be the Messiah of Whom God had spoken through the mouth of all His prophets. The name of this Jew was 'Yeshua.'

"Many Jews were deceived and misled, and they honored Him as the Son of God. The whole land of Palestine was stirred. His influence over the people increased rapidly. His followers waited day after day for Him to proclaim Himself king over Israel and make His disciples rulers and princes of His world empire. But the wise men of that time saw in His teachings and His influence over the people a great menace for the nation. They foresaw that if the Romans should gain knowledge of this movement they would come in larger numbers and would destroy the glorious city of Jerusalem and the gorgeous Temple, the pride of the whole nation.

"Therefore a special council of the wisest elders at Jerusalem was called to session. The object was to find a way to prevent the approaching danger. Sane advice was given by the noble and prudent high priest, Caiaphas, 'that it was expedient that one man should die for the people, and not the whole nation perish.' His good advice was accepted by the majority of the members of the council, and there and then it was determined that the impostor, 'Yeshua,' must be killed. The latter was at that time in Galilee with a large number of His disciples, but He was expected to come to Jerusalem for the Feast of the Passover.

"The plot was a wise one and successful, too, though the impostor and His followers knew about it. However, He was not afraid. He counted evidently on the support and protection of the masses. But the elders exercised great care in accomplishing their plan. Fearing the masses might rise to His defense, it was resolved that He should be arrested at night. One of His disciples, who was discontented with his Leader, rendered a great service; he promised to betray his Master.

"Judas was the name of this follower of the deceiver. On the appointed night, he led the men and officers who were sent by the priests to a secret place in the Garden of Gethsemane where 'Yeshua' often spent the night with His disciples. There He was taken that night. His followers, however, instead of defending Him after His arrest, fled and hid wherever they could.

"The high priest, together with the elders and all prudent people, did all they could to get Pilate, the Roman governor at Jerusalem, to sign the death sentence of 'Yeshua' that the Sanhedrin had already passed. Our fathers had in those days not even a right to execute their own criminals. Oh, the depth of shame and humiliation the Jews were in!

"When finally the death sentence was confirmed by Pilate, they led 'Yeshua' outside of Jerusalem and there they nailed His hands and feet to a wooden cross with large nails. There He died.

"His body should have been thrown out into the Valley of Hinnom for the dogs, as is fit for a criminal, but a fatal mistake was made through the carelessness of our elders. One of His secret followers who was even a member of the Sanhedrin went to Pilate and pleaded for the body to take it from the cross, and before the council could take the proper steps, this disciple had taken His body from the cross and buried it in his own tomb in his garden near Jerusalem, as is fit only for decent, wealthy people.

"After that was done it was too late for the elders to do anything without acting against the rulers. But they did remember well that 'Yeshua' had said to the people before He died that if He should be killed He would rise from the dead. In this they saw a new calamity for themselves and their people. They feared that His associates would steal His body, carry it to another place, and proclaim the news of His resurrection, as He had foretold. To prevent this, they sent a delegation to Pilate to tell him about their apprehension and to secure a detachment of soldiers to guard the sepulcher.

"The guards were posted near the grave. All calmed down and the people commenced with the preparations for the joyful Feast of the Passover. Yet His disciples did not sit and fold their hands. They got busy. One night they succeeded in putting the guards to sleep or else frightening those superstitious *Goyim* so badly that they were paralyzed with fear. When they came to themselves, they found the seal on the grave had been broken, the large heavy stone rolled away from the opening, and the grave was empty. The corpse was taken and nobody knows to this day what happened to it.

"His followers then spread the news throughout Palestine that 'Yeshua' had arisen from the dead. Later they carried this word all over the world. They affirmed they had seen Him after His resurrection and He had spoken to them. They even said they had seen Him ascending up to heaven as the Son of God.

"Of course this is all nothing but a clever deceit and no one of the wise and circumspect among our people have believed it nor do believe it today."

Thus Rabbi Weinberg finished his story about "Yeshua."

Judith had been listening breathlessly to the interesting history of "Yeshua." After a few minutes of dead silence, she lifted her eyes to her grandfather and asked in a subdued voice trembling with emotion: "But what if 'Yeshua' WAS indeed the Son of God, the promised Messiah sent to Israel?"

Recalling the words of the rabbi who a few days ago had argued with her grandfather, she added,

Happy Days of Childhood

"What if He died as the Lamb of God for our Jewish people and for all who live on earth?"

Mr. Weinberg jumped to his feet at this question. Glaring at Judith with furious eyes, he forgot she was only a thirteen-year-old girl and not a rabbi. Beside himself, he shouted: "Who has put such blasphemous thoughts into your head? Where is it written that 'Yeshua,' the son of a poor carpenter of Nazareth, is the Messiah of the Jews? The Messiah must come from the worthy, honorable family of David."

Pale and trembling with fear, Judith sat before her enraged grandfather. Never before had she seen anyone so terribly angry. Still she could not understand what it was all about — what had made him so very angry. She had said nothing that could have offended him to such a degree.

Looking at the frightened face of his grandchild, Weinberg came to himself again. Trying to undo his harsh action, he added in a soft, caressing voice: "My precious child, throughout my whole life I have had to battle against various heresies that threatened our nation. I am tired of it, and every mention of any heresy provokes me greatly, especially when anybody mentions this 'Yeshua,' whom the heretics worship as their Messiah, the Son of the Blessed. I know that you called him by this name through ignorance, not knowing what you were doing. Nevertheless, it is not good, my child, that you compare this impostor with our glorious Messiah, Whose appearance we await impatiently in the nearest future."

"Dear Grandpa, I do not know whether He was the Messiah or not, but I feel so unspeakably sorry that they killed Him, the innocent one, just as they killed the innocent lamb in Egypt. That's why I asked if

He might not have been the Messiah. Perhaps the people made a mistake."

"No, Judith dear," answered the rabbi. "The wise rabbis of that time could never have made such a mistake. And even if it had happened, there has been enough time and opportunity to realize it, to repent and to correct the error by accepting His teachings."

"Were any of His teachings left after His death?" inquired Judith, anxiously.

"Oh, yes, there is a book His followers claim contains His teaching. But this book and His disciples are the best proof that He was not the Messiah, the Son of the Blessed, but simply an impostor."

"How is it possible, Grandpa, that His disciples themselves say that He was not the Messiah? I cannot understand this."

"Oh, my child, you are surely more curious than your mother has told me. Evidently you want to know everything at once. This, however, I can explain to you easily, and I hope you will understand. Look around you and watch the people among whom we live. All people here in Russia, as well as in the other European countries, and in America, call themselves Christians, that is, followers of 'Yeshua,' with very few exceptions. But how these Christians do hate us, the Jews, while they are the followers and worshipers of a Jew! There have been times when they have massacred the Jews by the tens of thousands. Even today the feeling is no better. I have lived through several Jewish pogroms here in Russia when they killed Jews without cause or guilt on their part.

"And whatever these Christians are yet preparing for our nation in the future is known only to the merciful God. Only a few years ago a book came off

Happy Days of Childhood 29

the press bearing the title, *The Protocols of the Elders of Zion,* written by some dishonest, degenerate individuals. In this book the great accusation is thrown against the Jews that we are striving to destroy all governments of the nations and that we are creating chaos and revolution. We are accused of being the cause of all suffering in this world. This book has already called forth several pogroms and who can tell what its effect in the future will be?

"This is all brought upon us in spite of our loyalty to the countries in which we are scattered, for we have brought much benefit and blessings to these countries.

"Lately the government itself has devised the so-called 'Bellis Trial.' A group of degenerates had killed a boy by the name of Andrew Youshenski at the time of one of their debaucheries and now the government attempts to put the guilt upon Mr. Bellis, whom, as a representative of Jewry, they accuse of having killed the boy in order to get the blood of a Christian for Jewish rituals.

"Through this trial attempts are being made to fix the accusation upon the Jews that we do secretly kill Christians to obtain their blood for our religious rituals. This all is done for the purpose of instilling hatred against us into the masses to our own destruction. And all this is done by the followers of this 'Yeshua' — the Christians.

"If 'Yeshua' had been the Messiah of the Jews, He would have taught His followers to love our people. But this is not all, my child. They even hate one another. At times they have had the most cruel and bloody wars, one Christian country against the other. They have killed each other in large numbers. They have burned each other at the stake and cursed each other with the most horrible curses. They have destroyed whole cities and countries. These Christians have exterminated millions of their own fellow-Christians during the centuries. And frequently it has been done solely because some of them thought that others did not believe in 'Yeshua' as did they and that the others misunderstood and misinterpreted His teachings. From this one can conclude that His teaching brought nothing good and failed to make His disciples better men and women. They remained rude, bloodthirsty Gentiles as they were before, hating one another unto death."

"Oh, how terrible!" whispered Judith. "What horrible people are His followers. They are just as bad and cruel as the Jews were when they crucified 'Yeshua.' They are not like Him at all. I would never want to be the follower of anybody if that makes the people so cruel and heartless. If His teachings do indeed make His disciples hate the Jews and kill each other, then of course He never could have been the Messiah of the Jews. You were right, Grandpa, in being angry with me. You see I did not know anything about His bad followers. Please forgive me for entertaining the thought that He might have been the Messiah. I want to serve the God of my fathers and be true and faithful to Him all my life!"

At this Judith threw her arms around the neck of her grandfather and covered his face and his long, snow-white beard with kisses.

"I realize now that Judith should have known this before," said Mr. Weinberg to his daughter-in-law, who had quietly watched the two. "I had never suspected that such serious thoughts troubled her young mind."

The gorgeous sunset colors had vanished long since and the air had become cool.

"Now, children, it's time to go to bed, or Judith will keep us here until morning with her curiosity. She makes Grandfather too tired," suggested their mother.

Wishing each other a good-night, all retired. It was some time before Judith could sleep. Her grandfather's narrative about the life and death of "Yeshua" and His awful followers who killed each other and hated the Jews, filled her mind and kept her awake.

"No, He never was the Messiah of the Jews," she decided, "and Grandpa was right when he argued with that rabbi." She fell asleep at last.

Judith was satisfied. She now knew about the things that had interested her most. The life in the open and the love of her mother and the others who surrounded her soon dispelled her serious thoughts about God and "Yeshua." On Sundays and holidays her father came away from his business in the city for a happy visit with his family.

So the days passed quietly and peacefully. Twice during the summer the rabbis repeated their visit. Again they passed whole days and sleepless nights in discussions and quarrels. Judith noticed it, but she was no longer sufficiently interested to listen. When she heard their heated disputes, she concluded they were quarreling about "Yeshua." She was glad her grandfather was wise and able to prove to the others that "Yeshua" was NOT the Messiah.

"How fortunate that there are such strong and faithful defenders of our father's faith," was her comforting thought at such moments.

II

REFUGEES

The World War — The Flight from House and Home — The New Home

A FEW YEARS had passed after the events described above. It was the beginning of the year 1914, the fatal year for Europe. Unusual uneasiness and tension were already felt during the first months among the officials and even the inhabitants of the frontier cities. Business was slow. Everywhere the people were talking about the awful cloud of war hanging threateningly over Europe. The Weinbergs, who lived near the German border, felt very uneasy. They could not even decide to leave the city this spring and go to see their old parents.

Finally the fearful day came; on the first of August the hurricane of war burst over the country and soon the whole world was set on fire for many years. The German army crossed the almost unprotected Russian border and invaded the cities and villages. In endless lines, the Russian army was moving day and night from the interior to the border to defend their country. The peaceful inhabitants fled in haste from their dearly beloved homes, not being able to take even the most necessary things with them. In great masses they were moving along every road toward the interior of the country, anxious to leave as fast as possible the territory stricken with the terrors of the war.

Refugees

No one even thought of taking the train for all railroads were taken for the transportation of the army and ammunition. Those trains returning from the battlefield were loaded with wounded, crippled young men who had given their life and health for the country. The government had its hands full to take care of the thousands of soldiers wounded at the battlefront, and it was impossible to do anything for the civilians. They were compelled to seek ways and means for their own safety. Like a living lava were the unfortunate homeless people moving along every passable road. Among these masses it was a frequent sight to see children cry for their parents and parents for their children as they lost each other in the stampede. In many cases they found each other only after many years, and a goodly number of them have never seen their dear ones again.

In the midst of these living lavas, there was the Weinberg family. Leaving their large possession to its fate, David Weinberg had been able to take with him only a few hundred roubles he happened to have at hand. Now he, with his wife and the three girls, were walking along the dusty road with the many thousands of other unfortunate refugees seeking to find a place of safety farther in the interior of the country. They felt just one desire in their hearts — not to lose each other, and to move forward as quick as possible farther away from the front and the awful shooting of the artillery that was rocking the earth.

After four days of strenuous and tiresome walking along the highway that runs parallel with the railroad, they succeeded, though with great difficulty, to board a passing freight train. Being entirely exhausted from the long walk and hungry, they were now able to rest at least somewhat, sitting on the floor near the open door of the car. The cars were badly thrown from one side to the other from the fast movement of the train. Every car was overcrowded with weary, homeless refugees. In spite of the fact that the sitting and standing in an overcrowded freight car was not comfortable, all passengers felt quite happy because they were now moving rapidly away from the front, nearer a safe place. Together in the car with the Weinbergs there were a number of children who had lost their parents and parents who had lost their children on the highway. These all were passing one station after the other not knowing where and for what they were going. Everyone was anxious to go farther away from the German border out of the reach of exploding shells.

David Weinberg and his family felt especially happy and grateful that they had not lost each other on the way, but their hearts were filled with grief at the thought of their old parents, who lived less than twenty miles from the border and who had hardly had time enough to leave their home before the German army took possession of that territory. But as it is very human to forget others if our own life is in danger, so it was with the Weinbergs. Anxious thoughts about the parents soon gave place to the worry over their own condition.

After having traveled some days by train, and feeling a little rested from the prolonged walk, the family began to consider the question of where to make their temporary home until the hurricane of war had passed and they would be able to return home again. At that time everyone was sure that the storm of war would pass over very quickly and that in a few months peace and order would be established.

After some consideration, the Weinbergs decided to choose the city of G—— for their temporary home. There were many Jews living in G—— and Mr. Weinberg had had some business with some of the merchants there. The recollection of this caused some sad feelings, as this brought to their mind the fact that through the loss of their property these connections were severed. Their thoughts wandered back to their big warehouses, the stores, the home and its surrounding property. Most likely it was all pillaged and ruined by the passing armies. Possibly the buildings even had been burned. It was only now that they began to realize the sad truth that they were left poor and homeless, like paupers, and that they would have to start from the very beginning.

There had not been much time to consider the past and take thoughts of the future when they fled from their home in haste with the multitude of others, nor during the four days' walk on the highway. Then it was only the fear of being taken war prisoners by the Germans and the worry not to lose any of the dear ones on the way that occupied their minds. But now as the train carried them past villages and cities where the people were still living in safety, they had ample time to think and grieve over their great loss. Together with this, the thought of their old parents troubled them more and more. Where were they now? Would they ever see them again? Perhaps they were not among the living any more. Rumors were spread among the refugees that the German soldiers did not make any prisoners but that they killed everyone after the most cruel tortures.

While thinking of the past, the hearts of Mr. and Mrs. Weinberg were burdened with the thought of the future. They had been fortunate to take a few hundred roubles with them, but what did that mean for the future? Part had already been spent while on their journey. The remaining sum was very small. How were they going to live? Judith had finished only two years in college, and the two younger girls were still in high school. Having always been determined to give their daughters the best education possible, it now grieved their parental hearts to thinks that their hopes would probably never materialize.

The girls were meanwhile amusing themselves. They seemed to be carefree and happy. Standing near the wide-open door of the car, they enjoyed watching the changing scenery of the country through which the train sped swiftly. Their lively talk and happy laughter filled the whole car and dispelled the sad expression from many a face, at least temporarily. Judith, however, left her sisters frequently and went to join her parents. Sympathetically, she looked at them with her beautiful dark eyes. She was now nearly sixteen. With her quick mind, she comprehended the situation in which her beloved parents found themselves. It was impossible for her to laugh and talk with her sisters without giving serious thoughts to the future. Yet she saw the future in a different, a much brighter light than her loved ones. From her early childhood she had known how God had helped her ancestors in times of trouble. She believed that God had not changed since, and if He had aided the people in ancient times, He surely would help in these days of sorrow and need.

Leaning against the door post, Judith watched the rapidly disappearing villages and cities. In her mind, she went back through the centuries to the land of Egypt. There she saw her forefathers as they in one night had girded their loins, put the primitive bags around their shoulders, took the staff in their hands, gathered their children about them and, leaving their possessions behind, had left the country in which they had lived for centuries.

Quickly and vividly, she compared their present situation with the past events in the history of the children of Israel. "We are now refugees just as were they. We, too, have left home and all that was dear to us," reflected Judith. "There our fathers were in the wilderness thousands of years ago, and we, too, are as in a desert, not knowing where to go or what to do. This vast country is a wilderness for us at present. But I trust that the same Jehovah Who went with our forefathers is with us now. And I hope that He will lead us, too, to a place where milk and honey flow."

"How great and wonderful is our God!" whispered Judith quietly. At this thought she lifted up her eyes to the clear, blue sky where the first bright stars were visible.

It was a pleasant summer night. But near the door there was a cool breeze, and therefore Judith went back to her parents, seating herself on the floor at the feet of her mother, leaning her head against her mother's knees. The mother embraced her darling daughter tenderly, caressing and kissing her. Judith felt big drops of tears falling on her face. It pained her very much to see her beloved mother in tears.

"You are crying, Mama, dear?" she asked softly. "Do you know, while I was standing there at the door a few minutes ago I was thinking of our forefathers in Egypt and what they had to go through. They were at one time refugees just as we are now. I was comparing our flight from home with their experiences. And I do believe, Mama, that the great and loving God Who helped our people in their time of distress will help us, too. Don't you think so too, Mama?"

"I have never thought of it yet, Judith, dear," replied the mother. "Papa, did you hear what Judith is talking about?" she turned laughingly to her husband, who sat near by with his head wearily resting upon his hands. "She is comparing our situation with the emigration of the Jews from Egypt, and she believes that Jehovah is going to bring us too into a land where milk and honey flow."

Mr. Weinberg could not keep from laughing. "Well, Judith, you are always our joy and a messenger of good news, but now you are even a good prophet. Well, well, you are thinking already of milk and honey, and only a few days ago while walking on the dusty highway our Judith was repeating more than anyone else, 'If only we had a drink of good, cold water.' Do you remember?" he asked, looking with tender love at his oldest daughter. She looked at him with a happy, bright smile.

"Yes, Papa, but do you remember that the Jews were asking for water in the wilderness, that they even murmured against Moses, and in spite of it, they got milk and honey? We are in a much similar condition, and we ask for water, and Jehovah will send us milk. I believe it, Daddy!" she added seriously. "I have been watching you and Mother while you were talking. You both were so sad that it made my heart very sorry for you. Why should we worry so much? Look here, we are all healthy and strong. We will start to work, and the Lord God will help us, and everything will be fine!"

"You are reasoning differently from Mother and me," said the father. "If we believe as you do, then of course all will be well. Mother and I were discouraged, but now you have strengthened us greatly through your faith."

The two younger girls had joined the group in the meantime, and both said in one voice, "Yes, Dad, we will work, too, to make a living."

"I am going to be your salesgirl in the store," declared Sara, the youngest of the three.

"And I will be a dressmaker. I like to do sewing," announced Ruth.

"Well, if we have to decide our occupation right here, then I will tell you, too, what I am going to do. Because I am very fond of little children, I think I will choose the profession of a teacher," added Judith, happily.

For over a week the Weinbergs had been on the way. First was the four days' walk, then the ride on freight trains, interchanging with weary tiresome hours of waiting at various railroad stations. But finally they reached their destination. Mr. Weinberg had sent a telegraphic message to some of his friends in G——, announcing their arrival. These friends had come to meet them at the station at their arrival, accepting the homeless refugees in a most hearty and friendly way.

The Weinberg family adapted itself very soon to its new environment of this city, which was largely populated by Jews. With the financial aid of his friends, Mr. Weinberg soon opened a dry goods store and when the winter came into the land, he found the family in nice, comfortable quarters, well supplied with all they needed. The three girls continued their education in local institutions of learning. The whole family felt quite at home among their friends in the business world of G——.

During the first three months, they had cherished the hope to return to their home in the west in a time not too far off. The father of the house was eagerly watching the papers for any news from the front. In the first days of the war, the people were almost sure that the war could not last longer than three months. But as time passed, they became convinced that it would be a stubborn and prolonged conflict. So the Weinbergs at last gave up their hope and became reconciled to the fact that they never would see their home again and that their possessions were irrevocably lost. They settled down for good, now. Mr. Weinberg gave himself with more zeal to his business, while the girls studied diligently in school. The mother was busy in the house, and the girls helped her faithfully after school because none of their servants had come with them and they were not able to hire a maid after the loss of their means.

Two years had passed. The Weinbergs had become permanent citizens in the city of G——. In their business, they had been very successful. It was now standing firmly without the financial support of friends. The girls had grown up, especially Judith, who was the pride of the parents and the favorite of the Jewish society. With motherly pride, Mrs. Weinberg remarked occasionally to her husband that there was not a girl in the city who could compare with Judith.

The latter had finished college this year. Being the first student, she had received the gold medal. It had been decided that she would enter university the coming fall. However, circumstances compelled the parents lately to think sometimes differently about the future of the beloved daughter.

The Bernstein family had been their closest friends from the day of their arrival in G———. Mr. Bernstein was a merchant who had a large dry goods business. They had been very successful and prosperous. The two families saw each other frequently, and more than once had the Bernsteins expressed their wish and made known the desire of their hearts concerning Judith and Solomon. Nothing would please them more than if the two would join their lives in marriage.

Solomon, an attractive and talented young man, was the only son of the Bernsteins, and he had won the hearts of the Weinbergs the first time they had met. He had finished business college this year and was at present with his parents.

At first the Weinbergs tried to pass these friendly hints of the Bernsteins silently. Yet when they were alone, they often found themselves discussing this question. In Solomon, they saw the suitable husband for their daughter, and to no one else would they have given her more willingly. Watching them, they noticed that they were frequently together and that they loved each other. This all made them think much about their oldest daughter and her future.

One day in July Solomon called on the Weinbergs to ask the hand of Judith. David Weinberg and his wife had loved this young man from the first day of their acquaintance and, knowing that Judith was in love with him, they consented readily. The engagement was announced to their friends, but the wedding was not to take place until next spring.

Judith, Solomon, parents, and sisters all were contented and happy. Judith had put aside the thought of continuing her education and was going to stay at home with her mother until she had to leave her the next spring to join another family.

The heart of Mrs. Weinberg grew heavy at the thought of the parting from her darling daughter. She was so attached to Judith that she could not think of a life without her. However, she was comforted by the thought that her daughter was being given to such a worthy young man as Solomon, and at times her heart was filled with parental pride.

III

SEEK AND YE SHALL FIND

*The Longing of the Soul — Gospel Meeting —
The Evangelist — Christ, the Messiah —
Peace with God*

THE SUMMER had passed, and fall had come. The days were dreary and cool. The meadows and pastures, which had been so luxuriously covered with a carpet of beautiful flowers and grass, were now lonely plains covered with dry yellow grass. The nightingale was not singing any more in the woods near the city. Only the wind was ominously speeding through the tops of the bare trees.

Judith withdrew herself often during these days from the company of the others and went to the large city park. There she wandered at times for many hours among the trees watching the yellow and brown leaves that covered the ground and rustled under her feet as she walked over them. A strange pain filled her heart in these lonely hours. Where was the reason for this great, painful longing? What did the young soul crave for? Judith herself did not know an answer to these questions. She was loved by all, and she in turn loved her dear ones affectionately. What more did she want? Yet her young heart was longing in those moments for a higher love from above that never would change nor vanish.

The wind tore the last brown leaf from a tree near by, and it fell to her feet. Judith looked at it, and tears filled her eyes. She picked it up and, pressing it to her lips, kissed the withered dry leaf. She could not explain why she felt so sorry for it. It seemed as if something near and dear to her heart had died.

"Our whole life is like the life of this faded leaf," she pondered. "Today we are young — we love and are being loved — and tomorrow the cold wind of life blows over us and we fade, wither, and droop. The next gust of wind tears us loose from our branch of life, and like this leaf, we are falling to the ground and mingle with the dust. Perhaps someone's foot will soon walk over you, too, Judith."

She had been uttering the last thought, and she shuddered at the sound of her own voice. An awe filled her heart at such thoughts.

"You are a very queer girl," she scolded herself.

"But isn't our whole life composed of queer and strange things? There are many unexplainable phenomena and unsolvable mysteries. I wonder how my life will end. Is it possible that it is like this leaf that falls and decays? Or is there something behind the grave? If — then what is it? Many people do believe in the immortality of the soul and a life after death, but nobody knows anything about it — my grandfather, for example. Probably his hour has come long ago, and he has left this world already. Where is he now? He read and spoke much of God. Yet is it possible that if there is a God that He did not reveal anything about this eternal existence to men whom He created?

"Grandfather was certain that 'Yeshua' never rose from the dead. But I have learned since that some people think and believe firmly that He arose. They also believe that He will bring from the dead all those who believe on Him and that they will live eternally. This all is perplexing. Our world is full of puzzles. We are living as in a dream, or delirium. I wonder if the reason for the present longing in my heart is not in this mystery. Aren't these decaying leaves telling me of this mystery in their own language which, though I cannot understand with my mind, I feel with my heart?

"Where is the solution for it all?" asked Judith, and the echo quietly repeated her question, carrying it through the trees of the park.

"How dreadful it is here at the cemetery of dead leaves," she whispered, shivering, as she turned. She left the park and went home.

Judith had lately frequently been occupied with similar thoughts. Her soul was longing for light, truth, and life. Sometimes she confided her troubles to Solomon when alone with him. He was not a fanatical religious Jew. In many things he understood her well. Although he had been brought up in the home of religious parents, he did not believe in God. Sharing many of Judith's ideas and ambitions with her, he could neither understand nor share her longing for God and her desire to know more about Him. However, he did not consider her thoughts heretical because they differed from the Jewish traditions. His cold unbelief grieved her at times, but she comforted herself with the hope that finally he would change and become a believer.

Day after day passed quickly. The fall had given place to the cold Russian winter. The vast steppes, pastures, and forests were covered with snow as with a white shroud. The pure white crystals of snow were filling the air, and slowly they fell to the ground as if they were eager to cover Mother Earth better and so protect her from the severe frost.

The Weinberg family was kept busy during the winter giving parties or visiting their friends on the long evenings. They forgot more and more about the loss of their former home and their large possessions, as they were happy and contented in the new place. Only Judith was pensive and melancholy. Neither theater nor other amusements could fill the emptiness and satisfy the desire of her heart. She went occasionally to the synagogue, but the services there seemed strange to her and did not touch her heart. She understood but little of what the rabbi or the cantor read.

At that time the desire grew in her to get acquainted with some other religions. There were besides the Jews, many Greek Catholics in G——, also some Lutherans, and a group of the Russian Protestant Church. Each group had a church, and Judith decided that she would go and attend some of the services. But she found it quite hard to carry out her decision. She was aware of the fact that with her going even once to one of these churches, she would offend the religious feelings of her parents. Besides, her own conscience troubled her. She was not sure if it might not be a sin before Jehovah if she, a Jewess, would go to the church of people who honor the deceiver "Yeshua" as their God.

"Anyhow, if Jehovah is indeed omniscient, then He sees and knows my heart," she meditated. "Then He must know that I want to know and serve Him better. He will never judge me for the desire to know how other people believe and pray."

Judith now often remembered her fellow-student in college, Elizabeth Mirosh. She was the daughter of the pastor of the Russian Protestant Church and was a consecrated Christian girl. Thinking of her, Judith recalled that she had always been an exemplary, modest student. Judith had loved her since she met her first. There was only one thing that separated them. Elizabeth had used every opportunity to speak about "Yeshua" or to give Judith a book of tracts about Him. All the other Jewish girls in college had treated Elizabeth with contempt, calling her when among themselves in their own Jewish language, an "idolater" and a *Goyim*. Because of these girls, Judith had never been able to get closer to Elizabeth, though in her very soul she would have been willing to exchange all her light-minded girl friends for this one *Goyim*.

Judith had noticed that Elizabeth loved her more than the others. She recalled vividly how one day Elizabeth had looked at her lovingly with her pretty blue eyes and then said sorrowfully: "I am so sorry because you do not believe in Jesus Christ, Judith, and that you cannot come to our gospel-meetings to hear about Him. But I want you to know that I have been praying for you since I have known you. I am asking the Lord to open your heart and give you faith in Him, and I do believe that He will answer my prayer, and some day you will become His disciple and my beloved sister in Christ."

These words had sounded very strange to Judith at that time. She had even been provoked and had felt the desire to tell Elizabeth that this "Yeshua" had been a deceiver and a false Messiah, but somehow she could not do it, as she realized how whole-heartedly

Elizabeth believed in Him and how sincerely she spoke about it. She had only said that she, being a Jewess, could not and would never believe in "Yeshua."

Sitting in her cozy, comfortable room, working on fancy embroidery, Judith was in a reminiscent mood. Finally she said to herself: "How strange things are! Evidently not all followers of 'Yeshua' are alike; not all hate the Jews and kill each other, as my grandfather told me. Elizabeth told me once that many members of her church, who had been conscripted for the army, were cast into prison because they refused to take up arms and kill their fellow-men, for she said that 'Yeshua' had taught to love one another, even the enemies. Here is certainly something I cannot understand. Anyhow, I am not a child any more that has to believe what others tell him. The best is to investigate and to find out for myself," she concluded, lifting up her eyes from the embroidery.

But how could it be done? It was much easier to decide than to accomplish. One incautious step might cause a violent storm, not only in the home, but in the whole Jewish society.

"They might even consider me an apostate," Judith considered. Should she speak to Solomon about it? Perhaps that would be the best thing to do. But how would he accept it? At this thought, her face was lightened by a happy smile. She had been confiding all her thoughts and troubles to him, and she was sure he would understand her and would know a way out of her difficulties. Though she became more and more convinced that he did not believe in anything, she was certain that he would never interfere with or try to destroy her faith in God.

Seek and Ye shall Find

This day seemed endless to Judith. She could hardly wait until evening when Solomon would come as usual to see her, at least for a few minutes. She waited impatiently for him, being anxious to tell him about her desire to acquaint herself with the religious belief of others. Finally, at eight o'clock, Solomon came with his parents. Soon the party divided into little groups. Sara and Ruth, who had not finished their education yet, had chosen a comfortable corner to study undisturbed. The men discussed business matters and the latest events in Russia, while the two mothers talked about their homes and families and the city news. Only Judith and Solomon were engaged in a conversation that was foreign in the home of the Weinbergs.

After the arrival of the visitors, Judith had smilingly said to the parents: "Tonight you are going to be deprived of Solomon's presence for the whole evening. We are going to have a very important conference."

"You aren't going to plan to run away from us and go to America, are you?" asked her father, laughingly.

"No, no, Daddy, but there is something far better than going to America, something far more interesting than that," replied Judith, turning with a happy smile to Solomon.

"Come, Solomon, let us leave them talking about their business. You are mine for the whole evening."

"All right, Judith, I am at your command, and I am ready to listen to all your plans and all you have to tell me. If you plan to run away, then we will go together, won't we?"

"Certainly, I would not go without you."

With these words, Judith and Solomon went into the adjoining room, where they found a cozy corner.

Being alone here, Judith opened her heart and told Solomon all that troubled her mind.

"You know, Solomon, I have indeed a very serious petition tonight. I want to tell you what has been in my mind lately. Therefore, please listen seriously from the very beginning, and then forgive your girl should my desire seem foolish to you. Will you promise in advance to forgive me?"

"Certainly, Judith, dear," replied Solomon. "You may tell me everything that troubles your little head, and I will be glad to help you if only I am able to. For the two of us, it should be much easier to untangle the difficult questions than it is for you alone."

"Well, then, I shall tell you all. You know, Solomon, that I do believe in God with my whole heart, and I am anxious to keep this faith forever."

"Yes, Judith, I do know it, and you may be assured that your Solomon has nothing against it. On the contrary, I appreciate your genuine faith greatly, and often I think how lucky you are that you can believe in God so simply and whole-heartedly. Perhaps some day I shall change and my convictions will be like yours."

"I do hope very earnestly that this will happen some day, Solomon. But now listen. We know well that all religious Jews consider all other religions pagan, and our religion forbids us to have fellowship with the followers of other religions. You are smiling. The talk of your girl seems foolish to you, Solomon. But it is not so with me. For me this is a very important, serious question, and not foolishness."

"My dear Judith, your words did not cause the smile, but I was thinking how silly people are. They have created for themselves gods and religions, and now they pride themselves with these gods and religions, exalting themselves one above the other, and even destroy each other because of it. I do not believe in the existence of God, and the reason for my unbelief is the many various religions. For if there is a God, then there is only One, and there should be only one religion among all nations. However, we meet with hundreds of gods and beliefs. And the pity is that each religious society thinks that its religion is the best and the only true one. This fact makes me think that each nation has created its own god and religion according to their own understanding and to the circumstances under which they live. I say again, you are lucky, Judith, that you are able to believe with such child-like simplicity. But never look down upon others as did our forefathers, and as all religious Jews do even to this day. If there is a God, then He must be the God of all nations and not of the Jews only."

Judith's eyes, full of tender love, were fixed on Solomon's as he spoke these words with great earnestness.

"That is just what I wanted to talk to you about this evening, Solomon," she said warmly. "This is what has burdened my heart for a long time. I have been taught from my early childhood to love the Jews and the Jewish religion only and to look down upon all other people as being *Goyim,* and upon their religion as being an abomination to God. But now I am not a child any more that I have to believe blindly what others tell me, and I want to know why I must love the things I was taught to love and why I should hate the things I am told to hate. Am I right or wrong?

"Why I must love my people and its religion, I do know well. I have heard and read much about it. I know the history of our nation and I know and believe that our religion was given us by God Himself, though there is much in it that I cannot understand yet. But here we live in the midst of other people. With many of them we come into contact daily, and all these people believe differently from us. There are not a few very good and worthy people among them.

"Because of these facts the desire is growing in my heart to get closer acquainted with the religious belief of the people around us and to see their services and worship that I might be able to judge for myself. It seems to me that it is not quite right to study the religions of others just from books. A much better way is to do it by watching the lives of its adherents. But I know too well that my parents would be very much displeased should I go to any of the churches here to attend the service. That is why I wanted to tell you all this and ask your advice. I could never ask Mother and Dad about it, for they would be horrified to know that I had such thoughts. You are to be my judge. If my conception of these things is wrong, then let's forget this conversation. I had to open my heart to somebody."

Solomon had been listening attentively all the time. Judith's suggestion to visit other churches seemed very strange to him, though he himself did not believe in God. For several minutes he sat quietly without moving. His head was resting upon his hands. Judith was alarmed. She watched the changing expression of his face.

"What is it, Solomon?" asked Judith, breaking the tense silence while putting her hand upon his. "Are you, too, thinking that your girl is a heretic, an apostate from the faith of our fathers?"

"Oh, no, Judith. I have told you what my opinion is of all religion. It only sounded so unnatural as you spoke of attending services in churches alien to the Jews. Why these feelings came over me I cannot understand myself. Probably it is the result of the influence of those views and opinions under which I was brought up before I commenced to think for myself.

"I think it is best to keep this, our conversation, secret between the two of us; don't you think so too, Judith? Do not speak to your parents, neither to mine of it, for God knows what thoughts might enter their heads should they know about it. Most certainly it would worry them greatly. As far as we two are concerned, I think it would be interesting to go some day to some of the churches and cathedrals and see and hear what's going on there. I have never been interested in such things, therefore I have never been anywhere except in our synagogues, and there I went only because I did not want to hurt the feelings of Dad and Mother."

Solomon and his parents had left, and Judith went up to her room, But sleep fled from her eyes. Mixed feelings of joy and sorrow filled her heart. While she had watched the changing expression in Solomon's face as she told him of her plans to visit the Christian churches, she had assured herself that he was not yet a hopeless atheist. There was still, though unconsciously, a love for the Jewish religion in his heart, although he said that he did not believe in God. There was still hope that he might become a believer. This revelation was the source of great joy to Judith. On the other hand, she felt depressed as she recalled his words concerning the belief of the other people that they were "alien to the Jewish religion." These words made her fear that Solomon might be a strong fanatic some day, although at present he was displeased with the attitude of the religious Jews and their leaders toward the Christians and their religion. This alarmed her and filled her heart with quiet grief.

"O Jehovah!" exclaimed Judith after meditating on the discourse of the evening for a long time. "If Thou art omnipotent and omniscient, then Thou knowest all the thoughts of my heart. Let me comprehend Thee and Thy truth. Do not leave me erring in ignorance and darkness."

"What a strange girl am I," thought Judith as she prepared herself for the night. "Since I was a child I have bothered Father, Mother, and my Grandfather with my questions about God, and now I start to annoy Solomon with them. What will he think of me after our talk this evening? Well, I do not care, for I know that he loves me, and if it was silly of me to talk the way I did, he will forgive and forget. Everybody is talking and doing some foolish things sometimes in life."

Two months had passed. One evening the Weinbergs had gone to see Solomon's parents, and now the four were engaged in a very serious conversation. A grave expression was upon their faces. Mrs. Weinberg was frequently wiping the flowing tears from her eyes. Solomon was sitting on the other side of the room. His head rested heavily on his hands, and painful sighs escaped his breast.

"I have no influence over her any more," said Judith's mother mournfully, after a short silence, struggling to keep her tears back. "Neither has her father. We have lost our heads and do not know what to do.

The peril of our child is almost unbearable for us, and we have to be ashamed to show ourselves anywhere among people. She seems to have either lost her mind or she is bewitched. To all our pleas and threats, she replies the same thing, 'I know it's so hard for all of you, and that pains me so, but surely I cannot give up that which is holy and sacred to me. I must obey God rather than men.' Oh! oh!" sobbed Mrs. Weinberg. "Judith, Judith, my poor child! Is it possible that you are lost for us all who love you so dearly?"

All were sitting with bowed heads, and the tears were flowing freely.

"I, too, am helpless and cannot do anything with her. Yet I do still hope that all will be well one day. Three times I have tried to speak to her. I have pleaded with her to leave this delusion for my sake and for the sake of her parents and her nation. She has, however, only one answer, 'No, Solomon, I cannot give it up. I love you and my parents dearly, and also my nation, even more than I ever have before. But I shall never deny my Savior for your sakes, for that would be the most unnatural and indiscreet act I could ever do. That would be worse than committing suicide, for our body is going to die some day anyhow. To reject and give up my Redeemer would be committing suicide of the soul.'

"Her talk was so strange to me that I did not even know what to answer her. I think she has been brooding over religious questions too much lately, and it has affected her nerves. To make matters worse, this terrible man appeared who made such an awful impression upon her sensitive heart. Yet I still cherish the hope that she will get over it and all will be as it was before."

This family conference in the home of the Bernsteins was caused by the following occurrence:

About three weeks after Judith had told Solomon of her intention to visit some of the Christian churches and cathedrals, an evangelist had come to the city of G—— and was holding meetings at the Russian Evangelical Church. Printed announcements of the meetings were posted all over the city. These posters contained a special invitation for the Jews. The author promised that his meetings would be of great interest and benefit to the Jews. Although these announcements were torn off and destroyed as quickly as possible by Jews and some so-called Christians who were enemies of the gospel and did not want that others should know of these meetings, Judith and Solomon happened to see some of them as they took a walk on one evening.

"There we are, Solomon," said Judith, looking up to Solomon with a smile after she had read the poster. "Recently we spoke of going to some of the Christian churches to see how they worship, and now they even invite us to come. There is a Russian saying that 'An uninvited guest is worse than a Tartar,' and I reckon it is just as bad if one is invited and does not go. I suppose many of our Jews will go to these meetings, and naturally nobody will be surprised to see us there. Even if our parents should learn about it, it would not excite them much. This is a wonderful opportunity, isn't it?"

"I guess you are right," answered Solomon cheerfully. "This time I do fully agree with you. I am very anxious myself to hear what this man has to say to the Jews or about them. We shall go tonight. I will call for you about half-past seven and we shall satisfy your curiosity tonight that you have nourished for so long, though I am just as curious by now."

The large hall was overcrowded when Judith and Solomon entered. Looking around, they noticed that about twenty Jews whom they knew were present. The two had just entered, as two men, strangers to Solomon and Judith, arose from the last pew, offering their seats to the newcomers while they themselves remained standing near the door. The courtesy of these strangers surprised Judith greatly, especially as they seemed to be plain working men. Thanking them for their kindness, the two took the seats.

In a few minutes a small choir began to sing. The tune as well as the words of the hymn touched Judith's heart at once. There was something in it that seemed near and dear to her soul. One felt the simplicity and heartiness in it. Listening attentively, Judith could not help thinking: "These people surely believe in and worship the same God as we Jews, only here is more simplicity and reverence."

The choir sang:

O Jehovah, through the billows
And through the wilderness lead us.
We are weak — but Thou art mighty.
Press us closer to Thy breast.
With manna from heaven, manna from heaven,
Feed us now, O Lord, our God.

Oh, release Thy streams from heaven
From the rock of holy gifts,
Let Thy glorious fiery pillar,
Go before us, night and day.
Lord, our Savior; Lord, our Savior,
Be Thou near us; be our shield.

We are standing near the Jordan.
Lead us through the waters, Lord.
Bring us to the plains of Canaan
Where Thy people might find rest.
Songs of honor, praise, and glory
Shall ascend from thence to Thee.

Like an echo from ancient times, these words resounded in Judith's heart. The history of Israel passed quickly before her vision. She thought of the time when Israel was on her way to the Promised Land, being led by the strong and mighty arm of Jehovah.

The last words of the song were sounding through the hall. Judith was still sitting with her head bowed and her eyes were filled with tears. Solomon, too, had been listening seriously and thoughtfully.

After a short pause, the choir arose again and started to sing another hymn, the words of which impressed Judith still more than had the first hymn.

The hymn was:

The earth is trembling, and with flashing lightnings
Rolls the thunder from one end to the other.
The voice of God is thundering and calling,
"Israel, My people, hearken to Me."

> *Israel, you are building temples for Me,*
> *And the temples are sparkling with gold.*
> *In them incense is being offered,*
> *And the frankincense is burning day and night.*

Why do I need your temples,
The lifeless stone and dust of the earth?
I have made the earth and waters,
And the heavens are formed by my hands.

What is your gold to me, when in the deep,
In the womb of the sempiternal rocks
I have poured like the waters of the rain
The metal liquefied by fire?

Why the incense, when before Me
The whole earth from end to end
Is offering to Me the incense of
The fragrant flowers?

Why the fire? Have not I
Lightened the lights above your heads?
Am I not throwing the stars into the darkness of
*   the night*
Like the sparks of a furnace?

Thy poor gift is a worthless gift.
There is a gift pleasing to thy God.
Come before Him with it and, reconciled,
I will accept all your gifts.

What I need is a heart purer than gold
And a will firm in the work.
I need men loving one another
And those who will be true to Me always and
*   everywhere.*

Each word of the hymn cut deep into Judith's heart. The first song brought before her spiritual eyes the picture of the departure of the children of Israel from Egypt and their wandering in the wilderness, and the second reminded her of the later history of her people.

"Why are the sacrifices? Why the gold and the incense?" whispered Judith, unconsciously repeating the last words of the hymn. "Does He Who has created the heaven and the earth want us to take that which belongs to Him and bring it to Him as a gift as if it were our own? Yes, a heart purer than gold and an undefiled love one to another — that is really the best gift for Him," meditated Judith.

A swarm of thoughts filled her mind, but she had no time there to ponder over them. A middle-aged man with a book in his hand appeared now on the platform and took his place behind a table that was covered with a clean, white tablecloth. He had a pleasant, energetic countenance. For a few minutes he looked silently upon the audience with his penetrating eyes that seemed to look into the very depth of each heart present.

With a strong, firm voice he began: "Tonight we are having the first of a number of meetings in which we shall read and expound the Word of God according to the announcements you have read. But before we read from this precious Book — the Book of all books — given us by God Himself, I would like to invite all of you to join us in prayer to God that He might bless us and open our minds that we may understand His Word. We have no outward visible things for our worship, as you see; we do not need them because we know that wherever two or three are gathered in His name, there the Lord is present. The living, omnipresent God does not need dead things to remind us of His presence, for He Himself makes His presence known through the Holy Spirit. And if we rise to our feet to meet one of our fellow-men, how much more should we rise reverently in the presence of God as we speak to Him? Therefore, let us rise now in prayer."

The whole audience arose, with the exception of the Jews, who looked at each other not knowing what to do.

Seek and Ye shall Find

Finally some of them got hesitatively on their feet while the rest of them remained sitting. Being in the back seat, Judith had been watching those in front of her. She herself rose immediately after the invitation was given by the preacher. Solomon had followed her example.

A fervent, simple childlike prayer poured from the lips of the man behind the table. Like a child coming to his father with all his need, so this man approached God and spoke to Him in simple words. Judith had never before in all her life heard anything like it. She had often heard her parents read the Jewish prayers, and she herself had read them sometimes. But those prayers were written perhaps thousands of years ago. They were learned by heart and often repeated without understanding the meaning thereof. This was often a dead form without the quickening Spirit. But here this prayer did not sound like dead, memorized words. It was a pouring out of the heart before God, bringing the vital need of the hour to Him. This was a talk, full of faith and trust, of a man to the unseen, omnipresent God.

As the evangelist closed his prayer, all Christians in the audience joined him with their heartfelt "amen."

"Amen," repeated Judith, deeply touched. Solomon looked at her in surprise.

"What's the matter with you, Judith?" he asked sternly. "You are acting as if you were one of them. You arise when they do and even repeat their words. Watch our people. They all remained sitting silently with few exceptions. Is it right what you are doing?"

"I don't think I am doing anything wrong, Solomon. Should we not agree and take a stand for the truth although we hear it the first time in our lives?" answered Judith quietly. "In all that is being said and done here, I see and feel nothing but the truth."

Their conversation was interrupted as the evangelist called the attention of the audience to the Scripture he was going to read. He opened his Bible and read the fifty-third chapter of Isaiah where the life of the Lord Jesus Christ is depicted in a concise but very vivid way from His birth to His death on the cross of Calvary.

After the Scripture reading, he brought briefly the history of Israel and their wonderful hope for the coming of the Messiah before his hearers. He pointed out that according to prophecy the Messiah had to die first for the people, as the Lamb of God. Through His substitutionary death, the Messiah freed men from the bondage of sin and from eternal death, like as the lamb that had to die in that memorable night in Egypt to save the children of Israel from death together with the Egyptians and from the bondage of Pharaoh. But that which happened in those ancient times in Egypt was only a symbol, a type of that which God accomplished in later days through His Son, the Lord Jesus Christ, of whom the prophet Isaiah speaks. Of Him does the prophet say, "He was despised and rejected of men; a Man of sorrows, and acquainted with grief." He was as a lamb led to the slaughter, for He took upon Himself the sin of us all.

"Dear friends," continued the evangelist. "Let us now for a few minutes study the life of Jesus Christ, of Nazareth. Was He not despised and rejected by men? The scribes and Pharisees hated Him all the days of His life until they finally decided to do away with Him by nailing Him to the shameful cross. The heathen Roman soldiers made a crown of thorns and put it on His holy head; they spat upon Him, smote Him on the head with a reed, mocking and saying, 'Hail, King of the Jews!' Wasn't this humiliation? Was He not like a lamb led to the slaughter as He carried His cross to the place where they crucified Him, breaking down and falling under the heavy burden? He was indeed as a lamb, for He did not open His mouth. He did not complain, neither did He accuse His tormentors.

"This happened in times past, but the prophecy concerning the Lord Jesus Christ is being fulfilled even today. I see tonight in the audience a number of my Jewish friends. Oh, how greatly do I desire that tonight you would look into your past and the present. Are not your spiritual leaders continually putting the Lord Jesus Christ, the Son of God, and the true and only Messiah of Israel, before you as a false Messiah and deceiver? Is this not rejecting and despising Him through all the centuries?

"It is true that all religious Jews are still waiting for the coming of their Messiah to this day, but who will it be that will come soon? Who will this coming Messiah be? If we should begin to express our own opinions, we might easily fall into errors. God, who promised to send the Messiah, has foretold it, and He alone can give us an answer. Listen to what one of the inspired prophets of God says. We read in Zechariah, the twelfth chapter, in the last part of the tenth verse, the following words about the Messiah: ' . . . and they shall look upon me whom they have pierced; and they shall mourn for Him, as one mourneth for his only son. . . .'

"Whom have the Jews pierced in all their history? Who will come again to them? He whom they have pierced is Jesus, the Son of David. This had to be fulfilled according to God's plan of redemption. The blood of the innocent, blameless Lamb had to be shed for the salvation of Israel and the whole world, for the redemption of the people from sin and death. The prophets Isaiah, Daniel, and others have foretold this truth. This has been fulfilled, and now the other prophecies have to be fulfilled too. Israel shall look upon Him whom their fathers have pierced.

"Tonight the Lord is speaking once more to you, ye sons of Israel, and to all present . . ."

At this juncture a number of Jews arose noisily and left the hall. After quietness was restored, the evangelist continued:

"O children of Israel, to you first He sent His disciples with the preaching of the precious gospel after His glorious resurrection. And I, too, want to speak to you first after coming to this city. To you before all nations the Lord is willing to give peace and the joy of eternal life. He has great blessings for you that He promised even your father Abraham. Do not continue in your stubbornness to reject Him Who has shed His innocent blood for your transgressions and sin. Do not continue to put new thorns into His crown of thorns. Stop piercing Him with your unbelief and do not go on rejecting and despising Him. Turn to Him whole-heartedly in repentance and prayer.

"When will the blessed moment come for you who are present here that you will see Him Whom the hands of your fathers have pierced? When will you fall down at His feet Who was wounded for your sin, in tears of repentance? He is waiting! His eyes full of love are upon every one of you here in this solemn moment. He will bring you, the lost sheep of Israel, home to the fold. He is calling you tonight. Listen to what He is saying to you: 'Come unto me, all ye that labor and are heavy laden, and I will give you rest.' You who are burdened with sin and whose heart is without peace and rest, come! Come tonight, and He will give you rest and eternal life."

The last words of an earnest and warm invitation had been sounded. At the request of the evangelist, all present bowed their knees in prayer except a few Jews who had remained after the others had left. Many souls cried to God for forgiveness of their sins and for peace and help.

Judith had been listening with rapt attention during the whole message. Her eyes were filled with tears. Memories of the past had come to her while listening. She saw the picture of the country home of her grandfather, and very vividly she remembered the discussion of her grandfather with the two rabbis, friends of his, about "Yeshua" which she had overheard when a girl of thirteen. She had felt even at that time that the one rabbi was more right than her beloved grandfather, and now today she had the privilege to hear the living gospel about the Messiah, which was proclaimed here simple and clear.

An inner voice seemed to whisper all the time to her heart, "This is the immutable truth you have to accept. He is the Messiah, the Lamb of God, Who died for the Jews, for the whole world, and for you! We have to accept Him whom we have pierced. And you, too, Judith!" emphasized the voice.

"I, too?" uttered Judith's lips, as if answering the unseen.

Solomon was silently watching the expression of the face of the young girl. Three times he had suggested to leave the meeting and go home. He did not like the truth about Jesus Christ that was preached here openly and simply. But Judith refused to leave, asking him each time to wait a little while yet.

Although Solomon professed to be a modern unbelieving Jew it was evident that his infidelity was only on the surface; deep in his heart he had remained an orthodox Judaist. Hearing now the truthful story of the Lord Jesus Christ and of the attitude of the Jews toward Him, his real feelings grew stronger. He was very much displeased and hurt that Judith, whom he loved with all his heart, was so interested in what the man said and that she evidently considered it to be the truth. Judging by the expression of her face and the tears in her eyes, he was compelled to believe that she agreed with everything the man said.

When at the close of the meeting the Christians bowed their knees in prayer, Solomon felt that now was the moment for him to leave, for he thought it would be a disgrace for him, a Jew, to remain for the prayer of these people. He was much provoked by Judith's earnestness and urged her rather rudely to go home at once.

"No, Solomon," answered the latter in a whisper. "I cannot leave just now. The meeting seems to be nearly over, and I want to stay until the end."

Her heart was beating violently as she listened to the fervent prayers of many who prayed most earnestly for the salvation of Israel. Judith felt as never before that she, too, was a sinner. She, too, like the other Jews, had resisted and rejected the Lord Jesus Christ stubbornly until this day. She had considered Him a false Messiah and a deceiver and had humiliated and despised Him.

Seek and Ye shall Find

These thoughts flashed like lightning through her mind, and her heart was pressed with great pain.

"And what am I doing now? While all the others have reverently bowed their knees before Him, I am still obstinately sitting, not even rising to my feet."

"O God!" breathed Judith. "But what will Solomon, my parents, and my nation say?"

"Yes, but what shall He, the loving Lamb of God, say?" came the still, quiet voice.

Forgetting Solomon's presence and her parents, she suddenly threw herself on her knees, sobbing: "Forgive me, O Yeshua!" A burning, heart-touching prayer of repentance, kept back long, poured now from her heart and lips. She prayed first for herself, then for her loved ones and for her nation. Many of the remaining Jews looked in astonishment at Judith. Solomon sat at her side bewildered and frightened.

"O my Lord and my God, Yeshua, our Messiah!" prayed Judith; "henceforth I want to serve Thee with all my heart and soul. I want to be Thy servant and belong to Thee, and to Thee alone forever. Help me, O Lord, to follow Thee faithfully. Amen!"

"Amen! Amen!" said many voices with her.

The evangelist prayed after Judith had finished, giving thanks to the Lord for this sheep from the house of Israel which had come home tonight to her Good Shepherd.

By this time Solomon had come to himself. Grasping Judith by her arm, he pulled her up to her feet and pushed her rudely out of the hall. The fanatic Jew was now fully awakened in him. He was in such a state of mind that he felt like strangling her, whom he had loved so dearly, with his own hands or stone her on the spot because she had prayed to Jesus Christ calling Him her Lord. Judith complied meekly. She walked silently at his side like in a dream, not paying any attention to his rough conduct.

They did not speak a word all the way to their home. Solomon was sighing heavily from time to time. His blood was boiling with anger. His fury nearly choked him. He was angry at the preacher, the Christians, and Judith. The girl at his side felt just the opposite. Deep peace and rest were in her heart. She felt sorry for Solomon, for she realized that something awful was going on in his heart. Not to provoke him to greater anger, she thought it wise not to speak to him now.

Coming nearer to her home, she began to think of how her parents and the Jewish society would meet her after her experience of the night, for a number of Jews had witnessed her conversion. Most likely the news of it would be spread this very evening among the Jewish population of G——. Being hardly able to keep up with Solomon, who was walking fast, Judith called silently to the Lord for help. She asked Him, the omniscient and omnipresent God, to strengthen her for the coming hours and to give her much wisdom and patience for meeting her parents.

When they finally reached her home, Judith felt calm and at rest. Her silent cry had been answered by Him from whom she awaited help. An inner voice comforted her: "Be not afraid, Judith. Be firm, and I will be with you." The assurance that the Lord would not leave nor forsake her filled the heart of the girl with a joy that made her face radiant.

The parents and the two younger sisters of Judith were sitting in the parlor as Judith and Solomon entered. Without waiting for an invitation, the latter seated himself heavily on the chair nearest to him, not even taking off his coat. Holding his hat in his hands, he was sighing heavily. Judith passed quietly through the parlor, going to her own room.

Mrs. Weinberg's motherly heart felt instinctively that something unusual had happened. She walked over to Solomon and, putting her hand gently upon his bowed head, she inquired kindly, "What is the matter with you, Solomon? What has happened between you and Judith?"

Lifting up his head as if out of a dream, Solomon looked up to Mrs. Weinberg and shouted with a voice almost choking with anger, for he was not able to control himself any longer: "Ask Judith! Let her tell you. Well . . . no, don't, it's no use. She is an . . . apostate! She has disgraced us all. You, me, and our whole Jewish nation. I suppose the whole city knows it by this time."

Mrs. Weinberg was very pale when she took a seat on the chair close to Solomon. She did not know yet what had happened and looked bewildered at him. David Weinberg had not paid much attention in the beginning to Solomon but now he suddenly threw his newspapers aside. He had thought first that there was only a little misunderstanding between the two, as often happens between lovers. Hearing Solomon's words, he turned around and looked sternly at the young man.

"What has happened?" he asked harshly. "What has Judith done? Has she disgraced us all?"

"Yes, Solomon, tell us quickly what has happened to our daughter," urged the mother nervously. "Sara, please call Judith quickly. Why does she not come to us? Let her come and tell us what's wrong," she said, turning to her younger daughter.

The eyes of all were expectantly turned upon Judith when she entered the parlor. She was very calm. The only noticeable change in her was that her face, which was usually laughing and cheery, was now more serious and tense. She had just finished her talk with the Lord as her sister came to call her. Coming home, Judith had gone straight to her room, where she knelt down at the feet of her Savior pleading with Him to open the hearts of her parents, of Solomon, and her sisters, to accept Him, the Messiah, as their personal Savior.

"Help me now, my Lord," she said when Sara knocked at her door.

"Did you call me, Mother?" asked Judith, as she entered.

"Take a seat here," said her father, pointing to a chair. Judith obeyed silently. She felt that a serious moment had come for her, the moment when she must explain. She knew that now she had to confess openly her faith in the Lord Jesus Christ as the Son of God before her parents, sisters, and Solomon. This was not an easy step for one who had just been saved and not had time yet to come to herself and to think of it quietly.

"Listen, Judith," began her father; "we want to hear from you personally what you have done and what has happened between you and Solomon. We want to know of what shame and disgrace he is speaking that you have brought over us and our nation."

Judith had listened quietly with her head bowed. All eyes were fixed upon her, waiting for an answer.

Finally, after a short pause, she lifted up her head and, looking straight into the eyes of her father, she began with a quiet but firm voice: "Yes, Papa and Mama, something has happened; not between Solomon and me, but only with me. However, that which has happened does not disgrace you, nor Solomon, nor anyone else. I wish that all of you would experience the same, you and all our people, and all who live on earth."

"Speak quickly and clearer! Do not let us suffer any longer," interrupted her mother.

"Mother dear, I do not want you to suffer at all. I would much rather that all of you would rejoice with me. That which fills my heart at this moment, and that which has happened to me tonight cannot be told in a few words. Therefore, forgive me, please, Mama, that I am not able to express myself quickly. . . ."

"She . . . is . . . an apostate! She has brought reproach and shame upon us all," shouted Solomon, beside himself. He was so enraged that he could not keep quiet any longer for fear Judith would either try to defend herself or she would influence her parents.

"Apostate?" repeated the parents and the two girls in one voice, looking inquiringly at Judith.

"Yes, an apostate! Why are you listening to her? She is a Christian."

"A Christian? Our Judith a Christian?" asked the astonished parents and sisters again.

"Wait, Solomon," cried Mr. Weinberg, threateningly. Getting on his feet, he walked over to Judith. Looking at her severely, he questioned, "Is what Solomon says true?"

All held their breath. The father was standing before his daughter trembling with excitement and anger.

"O David, calm thyself. Let Judith alone. Let her tell us everything," interfered Mrs. Weinberg. He was an awful sight in his fury and even she feared him in this moment. In all the long years of their married life, she had never seen him in such a rage.

"Sit down, please, here, near to me," she said.

Breathing heavily, Weinberg took the chair at her side.

"Now tell us what you wanted us to know," she encouraged Judith, who was sitting very still and frightened. "You keep quiet, too, Solomon. Let her tell us what has happened to her this evening."

"Yes, Solomon has told you the truth. I do indeed believe in the Lord Jesus Christ as the Messiah of the Jews and my personal Savior and Lord," began Judith, with a firm, determined voice.

At the last words, Mr. Weinberg jumped up from his chair as if stung, but his wife kept him back.

"I had heard of Him occasionally in my childhood. Several times there was a hard struggle in my heart. I did not know whether He was the Messiah or not. I was unable to decide this question myself. I remember that I once asked Grandpa about it. The recollection of an argument I overheard is still very clear in my mind. Grandfather was debating the question about 'Yeshua' with two other rabbis. One of these rabbis proved that 'Yeshua' was the Messiah of the Jews. Tonight Solomon and I went to a Christian church for a meeting. A minister had come to their church from another city. While listening to the reading of the Scripture and his sermon, I became convinced definitely that Yeshua is the Messiah, the Son of the Blessed, whom our forefathers crucified, Who died as the Lamb of God for the sin of the world as it was foreordained. Being convinced of this truth, I gave Him my heart, and now am I, your daughter, His servant and follower from tonight and henceforth."

While she was talking, she had been noticing the changing expressions in the faces of her father and mother. She saw that a terrific struggle was in their hearts and that they were hardly able to control themselves.

At the last words of the girl, her mother grasped her head with both hands and commenced to weep and lament loudly. The father walked up and down wringing his hands. Solomon and the two younger girls wept quietly.

"Get yourself out of here and out of my sight!" commanded Weinberg, with a choking voice, trembling and pale with rage, pointing to the door. Judith arose and left the room quietly. . . .

IV

PERSECUTED FOR CHRIST'S SAKE

Enmity of the Parents — Vow of the Mother to Kill Her Daughter — Driven out from Home — Trusting the Lord

THE HYSTERICAL weeping of the mother lasted for a whole hour. The two younger girls had been sent to bed by the father. Solomon was still there, sitting with bowed head.

"With worry and tears we shall not be able to better the case," said Mr. Weinberg finally to his wife, after she became more calm. "Something has to be done. We three here are those who love Judith more than anybody else, and we all realize how perilous this step is that Judith has taken tonight; perilous for her, and unspeakably hard for us. But perhaps we can still save her with united efforts. I think it would be good if you would tell us calmly everything from the very beginning, Solomon. Lately you have been more with Judith than we, for we entrusted our daughter fully to you."

"Yes, that is right. Tell us all, Solomon," added Mrs. Weinberg.

Solomon had become his own self again, and he told the parents what he knew of Judith of late. He told them that Judith had been occupied very much with religious questions and that she had confided her thoughts to him. However, he had seen nothing wrong or dangerous in it; on the contrary, he had shared many of her thoughts and ideas. Tonight they had decided to satisfy her long desire and his curiosity by getting acquainted with some of the other religions around them. He said that his curiosity had been stirred through a deceiver from another city and his posters in which he invited the Jews to his meetings. And so it had been agreed to go to this Christian gathering.

After a short pause, Solomon continued: "And there in that meeting occurred something entirely unexpected. I would never have even dreamed of such an outcome. This evangelist proved to his hearers that 'Yeshua' had been indeed the Messiah of Israel, the Savior of the world. To strengthen his words, he quoted all the time our Jewish prophets, who speak about the coming of the Messiah. I watched Judith and noticed soon how attentively she was listening, drinking in every word. I tried repeatedly to get her out of the place but yielded each time to her petition to wait a little longer. I felt disgusted, and it pained me to look at her. I myself did not believe in God, but being a Jew I hated to see Judith to be so interested in the talk of this man, whose only aim seemed to be to accuse the Jews for crucifying 'Yeshua.'

"When the speaker finished his talk, he asked all present to bow their knees in prayer. And all did, with the exception of some Jews who remained evidently for curiosity's sake, for the majority of our Jews left the place after the close of the speech. I, too, arose, ready to leave, but Judith succeeded again in persuading me to stay.

"We were sitting in the back seat. Suddenly Judith dropped down on her knees after the prayer of one of the men, and she commenced to pray like those people did. All the Jews in front of us turned around and looked at us. I was stunned and did not know what to do. My heart was filled with grief. I was ashamed to lift up my eyes and to look at the Jewish friends. I felt disgraced and humiliated to the limit.

"After I came to myself somewhat, I lifted her up from her knees and, pulling her after me, I almost ran out of this horrible place. This is all I know and all that I can tell you about her. I am at a loss what to do now. The great love to Judith is struggling in me against that other feeling which has been called forth through the occurrence of the evening. I cannot give myself a clear account of what is going on in my breast. Until today I was not a believer in God and I was far from being a religious man, and therefore it is strange that I have the feeling that Judith has offended my deepest and most sacred feelings. This seems to indicate that there is a God and that the Jews are the only nation in the world who have the true religion given them by God. Judith has now become a conscious apostate from God and the religion of her fathers. She has at once thrown away everything and has trodden it under her feet.

"What shall I do? She is engaged to me, and our wedding is to be in the nearest future. It is impossible for me to show myself with her after this in our society, for a number of our Jews witnessed her hysterical prayer as she asked 'Yeshua' to convert our whole Jewish nation. And they saw me there together with her. . . . She is lost for me. . . . Lost forever. . . . We cannot love each other any longer; and even more — we cannot be even friends after this. . . . Oh!

How could this happen? . . . Judith, my dear Judith!" moaned Solomon, holding his head with both hands.

Judith's parents had been listening silently, crushed with their grief. The face of the father manifested a terrific inner struggle. The mother was crying. They both understood the feelings of the young man and they sympathized with him, for they suffered greatly in behalf of their daughter. As soon as Solomon finished, Mr. Weinberg arose, took the youth by his arms, and led him to his wife.

"You know, Solomon, that our hearts have been attached to you like unto our own son. We have loved you with all our heart and still love you. We know that you have fully returned this love. Now we have lost her who has united us so closely and whom we all have loved so passionately. We always hoped that she was going to bring us untold joy and honor in our life — and now she has brought such unspeakable grief and disgrace upon us that we do not know how to bear it or how to undo it.

"When she was sitting here an hour ago telling us that she had become a Christian, I felt something in me of which I could not give an account. If it had not been for you, Rachel, I do not know what I would have done to my child, although I do not know yet what to begin and what to do with her, I will not despair. Judith has surprised us from her earliest childhood with her quick mind and her deep questions, which were much too serious for her age. Besides, she has always been very impressive. Perchance we shall yet have the joy of bringing her back to the faith of her fathers. We three have now to make efforts and use all possible ways and means to influence her. For the first few days I think it will be best to leave her alone and to give her time to think over what she has done. I doubt that we would accomplish much with her through severity. I feel very sorry for my action tonight. In this respect, our nation has much to improve. But who can help it? It's our temperament! Let us try to reach our aim through love, through exhortation, and solicitation. We can, if necessary, invite our honorable rabbi to have a talk with her. And then it is left to be seen what to do further," finished Weinberg.

"Yes, you are right, David," agreed his wife. "We must do all we can to save our child, our beloved Judith. You, Solomon, will help us, won't you? You have an influence over her, for I know how affectionately our Judith loves you."

"Indeed I will," said the young man, having gained courage and hope again. "Please forgive my temper and my quick judgment. Perhaps my Judith is not lost for me yet, after all. Whatever depends on me will be done gladly for her."

It was about three o'clock in the morning when Solomon finally reached home. The remaining hours of the night were spent sleeplessly by him as well as the Weinbergs. Judith's conversion and her acceptance of Christianity was an unexpected blow for them. At the same time there was in the other part of the house another conversation quite different from the one in the parlor, one that was totally unknown in the home of the Weinbergs, a discourse not between men, but of a young girl with her God. When her father ordered her out of the room, Judith felt crushed with pain. She was used to being loved by everybody since she could remember and she had never been treated harshly. Now she felt for the first time in her life that she had lost this love. She saw that she was hated by those who were the nearest and dearest to her heart.

Judith loved her parents and Solomon with an unusually tender love, such as one very seldom finds. It was a pure, unselfish, genuine love and attachment. For several years she had known and loved Solomon. He was very dear to her. He had always been attentive, tender-hearted, and considerate. She knew that he loved her dearly. And now they had driven her from their presence.

The loving, always considerate father had looked frightful and threatening as he stood before her all trembling with anger. If mother had not kept him back, he would surely have killed her right there on the spot. At this recollection, the girl's heart was pierced anew with an unknown, indescribable pain. She felt suddenly helpless and lonely in this world. There was nobody on earth to whom she could go now with her almost unbearable grief. There was not a soul to whom she could run and on whose heart she could cry out the sorrow of her young heart. Mother, Father, Solomon, her dear sisters, and her nation, had cast her out for the Lord's sake. She realized that all bonds of love were now severed. She felt like one thrown into the raging waves of the sea from the deck of a ship, not having firm ground under her feet and no shore being in sight.

For a long time her subdued sobs filled the room. This was the first real grief in Judith's life. After the first crying spell was over, she arose from the bed on which she had fallen prostrate when she entered her room with the shock of being driven from the presence of her dear ones. Now she sat down on the chair near the window. It was a quiet night. The moon was shining peacefully. The bright stars twinkled and sparkled like diamonds. The girl's eyes, tired and swollen from weeping, were fixed upon the beautiful picture of the starry winter sky. Lost in contemplation, she sat motionless for a while.

"Thou are great and glorious in Thy creation, oh, my God!" uttered Judith in a subdued voice. She had become quieter, and a sweet peace began to fill her heart. Sitting there in the loneliness of the night, her whole life passed before her. She thought of the time when she was a little child, as she and her parents still lived in the West, in the part of the country that had been taken away from Russia through the war. She remembered the question that had troubled her for quite a while after her father had told her and her sisters the story of the past of her nation. These tales of her father had roused her childish mind and had awakened in her the desire to know more about God.

She recalled also that memorable discussion of her grandfather with his guests which she had chanced to overhear. And her discourse with her grandfather afterward came very vividly into her mind.

One picture of her childhood after the other had passed quickly before her eyes: Their flight from home in the beginning of the war; their traveling from the front to the city of G——; her first meeting with Solomon; and the following happy time of their love and engagement. It all seemed to her like a picture on the screen.

"That was a sweet dream, which has changed into cruel reality," pondered Judith. "But what now?

Persecuted for Christ's Sake

What has this reality in store for me? The dream is over. The picture of my life has changed entirely. Praise be to my Savior that He has led me out of this dream, for it is much better to awaken here on earth and to leave here with a real life than to open the eyes when entering eternity to meet there the tragic consequences of a spiritual sleep here on earth."

With her quick and alert mind, Judith considered all that was for and against her decision. She did not try to deceive herself with illusions of an easy life ahead. Lately she had been reading the Jewish Bible frequently. During these studies she was strongly impressed with the fact that all prophets, all true servants of God, had suffered much persecution, and not a few had met a martyr's death. And even Jesus Christ, the Son of God, had died the most cruel death, being crucified.

"If you want to follow Him and be His hand-maiden and disciple, then the same is awaiting you, Judith," she told herself. 'The first step is made. I suppose the whole city knows it already. Tomorrow all our people will wag their heads at me and point at me with their fingers. . . . But should I go back? . . . Oh, save me from such a thought, my Redeemer," pleaded the girl.

She arose and knelt down at the feet of her precious Savior and Lord and there in sweet fellowship and communion she forgot herself and her troubles.

"Thou knowest, my Lord, that from my early days I have longed and searched for Thee. In Thy great love and mercy Thou hast revealed Thyself to me tonight through Thy Word and the Holy Spirit. Thou hast washed and cleansed my heart with Thy precious blood. Now, Thou knowest that all have forsaken me for Thy sake. All my own whom I love dearly are hating me without cause and are driving me away from their presence. I have no friends here on earth, no one who will advise and help me in the struggle. I am alone, all alone. Thou knowest that I am only a weak girl and that I do not know Thy ways yet. Do not leave nor forsake me, O Lord. Do not let me err from Thy truth in my ignorance and weakness. Thou knowest what will happen to me in my future life. I do not know it. Help me, therefore, my dear Lord, in all circumstances of life, especially when I grow weak and weary and have no strength to withstand the temptations."

For a long time, her childlike, fervent prayer went up from her cozy room lighted by the silvery light of the moon. In the quietness of the night, Judith talked to her Savior as if He were visible at her side. She did not doubt it that He was there indeed, very close to her that very minute, and a great, deep peace came into her heart while she was praying simply and believingly.

"I am ready and willing to follow Thee everywhere. Thy will be done in my life from today and forever, my Lord and my God," was Judith's promise as she finished her talk with her Lord and Savior.

As she arose from her knees, her face, on which the moonlight fell, was radiant from inner joy and peace. Resting in her Redeemer, she soon forgot herself in a sound, healthful sleep. He to whom she had turned in prayer for help and strength sent His light-bearing angel to protect her and to guide and assist her on her way to the heavenly, eternal home.

Hard days commenced for Judith, days of trials, temptations, and persecutions from every side. Her parents and Solomon made great efforts to turn her away from the faith in the Lord Jesus Christ. They pleaded with her, invited her to go with them to theaters, dances, and other places of amusements, but she remained firm. She had turned her back on all things she used to enjoy very much, for she had found something far better. She considered it a sin against God, being His child, to go to the theater or to spend an evening in a dancing hall. She told them when they urged her to go, "There is no place for me where the Lord Jesus is excluded. I can be only where He is."

Solomon and her parents could not persuade her to do things she thought would grieve the Lord, and in proportion as they realized that all their efforts were in vain, they lost the hope of her return into the synagogue, and with it they lost their patience and self-control.

Several times Judith's mother arranged to stay at home alone with her; and with tears she pleaded, beseeching Judith to leave her present conviction, to repent, and to come back to the faith of her fathers. These entreaties and the tears of her dearly beloved mother were the hardest temptations and trials of her faith.

"Think of your future, Judith," began the mother one day. "You are deserting your nation entirely. The whole city looks upon you as an apostate. Have mercy on us! Don't you know how your father and mother are suffering because of you? Your sisters, too, who are now at the age when they should enjoy life, have to bewail your strange behavior almost daily. It is hard for them to show themselves publicly. They are being looked upon and treated with scorn and contempt for your sake. Last night they both came home crying. Ruth declared that she was not going to leave the house any more. Everybody is asking them where Judith is, and if the rest of us are not going to accept Christianity. O Judith, is it possible that our great suffering does not touch you the least bit? And look at your Solomon. What have you done with him? He meets mockery and derision on every step. You are not going with him to any place of amusement any more, and the poor boy has to sit at home all the time. If this is going to continue much longer, he will finally break your engagement and get rid of you. Who would want to have a wife that is an apostate—an heretic?"

"Dear Mother," replied Judith, "I do see and realize this all. My heart is aching for you, Solomon, and my nation. But, Mother, dear, how can I leave God and disregard His commandments? Should I take this step now then indeed would I be an apostate and my sin before Him would be great because it would be a sin committed knowingly and willingly. Doing this, I would exchange the eternal for the temporary and the heavenly for the earthly. I do not love you less now; no, I love you all much more than I ever did before, and I love Solomon very dearly, but I cannot go with him to these places of amusements. These places are an abomination before my Lord, my heavenly Bridegroom, and my desire is to be His true and faithful bride, yielded to Him more than to anyone here on earth."

Up to this point Mrs. Weinberg had listened patiently, but now she could not restrain herself any longer. Trembling with anger and almost choking, she shouted: "Faithless heretic! Apostate! You have disgraced our name, our old, honored family. You are

Persecuted for Christ's Sake

a black spot on our family and nation! Get out of here! I don't want to see you any more!"

With these words, she jumped to her feet and ran out of the room.

After this interview of Mrs. Weinberg with Judith, the two families gathered one evening to decide what to do with Judith. Afterwards it was agreed to invite the rabbi to talk to Judith. But this visit only resulted in the strengthening of Judith's faith in the truth of the gospel and in the error of the religious leaders of the Jews, who try with all their might to keep the Jews in darkness and ignorance concerning the Lord Jesus Christ and His gospel.

One day, about eleven o'clock in the morning, there was a sharp knock at Judith's door. She had been in her room for most of the time. There was no place for her to go, as the old friends had turned their backs on her and she was prevented by her parents from going to the church where she had been saved. They had forbidden it, and they saw to it that she could not go. Every step was carefully watched, and therefore she preferred to stay in her room.

She was doing some fancy embroidering as she heard the rap at her door. She expected that one of her parents or Solomon was coming once more to persuade her to come back to Judaism. Great was her surprise as she opened the door and saw the old rabbi before her. She knew at once what his mission was. Pushing a comfortable chair nearer, she asked him to be seated.

"My daughter, I have come today to ask you about a few things," commenced the rabbi, slowly. "Some time ago I was told that you have become disloyal to the religion of our fathers, which Jehovah Himself has given us and that you have gone over to the Christian, or rather heathen heresy. However, I could not believe that a member of the old, honorable Weinberg family could become an apostate until I heard it last night from your own parents. I am so sorry for you, my daughter, and I do hope that you soon will return into the bosom of the synagogue and to your people. Your youth and inexperience have caused you to slip and fall on the way of faith. But we, the synagogue and our nation, are willing to forgive you your sin for the sake of your worthy ancestors if you repent and confess your transgression. I shall be glad to help you to get out of this unpleasant situation. Tell me openly, my child, is it true what they are saying about you? If it is so — are you willing to repent and to ask for forgiveness of your great wickedness and sin?" asked the rabbi, looking kindly and fatherly upon the girl before him.

"Oh, yes, honorable rabbi, I am willing to tell you all, as it is," replied Judith. "As far as the religion which Jehovah has given us is concerned, I have not been disloyal to it."

The rabbi nodded graciously. He seemed to be pleased.

"About my going over to the Christian, or as you call it heathen heresy, I must tell you that I do not know anything of such heresy."

"But how is it, my daughter, is then all that I have heard a lie?" interrupted the surprised rabbi. "Is it possible that this all was just a mischievous trick of your youth? Even if that be so, my child, it is wrong and unworthy of you."

"No, rabbi, please listen to me until I have told you all. The fact is this. Long ago, even in my early childhood, I heard that there exists a Christian heresy that was founded by a Jew whose name was 'Yeshua,' of Nazareth. I was taught to hate this 'Yeshua' and His followers and to call them *Goyim*. As long as I was a child, I tried to do as I was told, thinking that this was pleasing to God. But as I grew up and commenced to think for myself, I came to the conclusion that if I love anybody I must know why I love, and if I have to hate I want also to know why I must hate. Am I right, worthy rabbi? You are wiser than I and can tell me if my conclusion is logical or if it's wrong."

"You are right, child. You are thinking logically," agreed the rabbi, looking at her in perplexity, feeling uneasy and alarmed.

"That's why I determined to use this rule in this case, that is, concerning 'Yeshua.' I said to myself, I will and must know why I should hate Him. To this end I started to study the Torah and the prophets and later also the life of 'Yeshua' through the Gospels. Through this reading I became more and stronger convinced that He was not a deceiver, as I heard insinuated since I was a little child, but the promised Messiah, the Son of the Blessed, Who had come to His people. Or in other words, the same Jehovah Who revealed Himself in different ways to Israel, took upon Himself the form of man, became flesh, and lived here as 'Yeshua' of Nazareth. This I do believe firmly, dear rabbi, and my prayer to God is that my dear parents, you, and our whole nation might quit resisting Him any longer and accept Him as your Messiah. I believe that sooner or later Israel will have to acknowledge

'Yeshua.' They will look upon Him Whom they have pierced, declares the prophet Zechariah."

The kindly expression of his face changed visibly, the longer the old rabbi listened to Judith. At first he became serious, then sparks of anger flashed over his face. Finally he jumped to his feet, his eyes sparkling with resentment and fury. Running up and down the room, he was nervously pulling his gray beard. He had become entirely unfit for any further discourse. Instead of exhorting the girl calmly and soundly and proving to her that she was wrong, he lost his self-control and even good manners. He commenced to curse the girl, all Christians, and even the Lord Jesus Christ.

"Such as she should be exterminated from the midst of our people," was the remark of the rabbi to the parents of Judith as he left the house. "She is lost irretrievably. There is no hope for her, and there is nothing to be done. It is a pity that the heathen laws of this country forbid us to execute our own laws and to stone her. She surely deserves it. My advice is that you remove her from your home and from our society as quickly as possible before she becomes a snare for many of our Jews. You are forbidden to have anything to do with her. She is an heretic, and our synagogue prohibits you to have any communication with such."

Judith became indeed more and more dangerous for her former Jewish friends. In spite of all the obstacles, she proceeded on her way. When she had a chance, she went to the Christian meetings, and she used every opportunity to witness before the Jews. She told them that Jesus Christ was the true Messiah of Israel and the Savior of the world.

Persecuted for Christ's Sake

Her parents and Solomon began to change their attitude toward her entirely as they saw that all their efforts to turn her from the truth had failed. They now became her greatest enemies and tyrants. The engagement with Solomon was broken. The synagogue and the parents of both sides demanded it. Judith was now surrounded in her own home by those who hated and detested her. She had been forbidden to leave the house. When friends of the Weinbergs came to see them, Judith was locked up in her room immediately. Her parents had spread the news among the Jews of the city that Judith was mentally unbalanced. When visitors inquired about the girl or expressed their desire to see her, they were told by the mother that Judith frequently had fits of a delirious rage and that it was extremely dangerous to let her out of her room or to go in to see her.

Judith often heard when her mother talked of her near her door to friends as being insane and dangerous. In such moments her heart seemed to break with unspeakable pain. The only comfort she found in those minutes was as she fled to her precious Savior in prayer. He strengthened and upheld her in the hour of severe trial.

Shortly after the visit of the rabbi, it was decided by the parents to do as he had advised and to expel Judith from their home. But they were going to speak to her once more. So one day the father and mother went to her to persuade her for the last time to come back to Judaism. Seeing that they could not move her with pleading, they began to threaten. As all their efforts failed to make her change her conviction, the father became provoked and said finally: "All that was possible for us we have done, trying to save you. We desired to save you from eternal peril — but all has been in vain. Instead of abandoning this heresy, you become more entangled in it. And this seems not to be enough for you, but you do all you can to entice your sisters and everyone you meet to accept this heresy. I cannot let this go on any longer. You must choose one of the two: either you renounce this awful heresy today or you are going to leave our house forever tomorrow morning and go where you like. You have until tomorrow to make your choice . . . This . . . is . . . our last word to you."

The life of Judith became harder and harder in the home of her parents, as we have seen. But these last words of her father were a terrific blow to her. There was a great struggle in her breast after her parents left her alone. She saw the gulf growing deeper and wider. Her nation had despised and cast her out long ago. Solomon had forsaken her. But now the hardest moment in her life had come. Judith had never thought of such a possibility. Although it was the inevitable consequence of her conversion to the Lord Jesus Christ, she had never admitted the thought that her parents would be able to treat her in such a way.

She had now to face and decide the hardest problem of her life, and it was far more than she, a young girl, had strength for. But He Who has promised to be with His own always, even unto the end of the world, was close to Judith in these dark hours. She was already used to seeking refuge in Him in moments of sorrow and trial, for such moments had been many since her conversion. The difficulties grew up before her like mountains. Being young, frail and lonely, she could go through victoriously only with His help and under His protection. And so, forgetting the past, she was pressing forward by faith, following in the footsteps of her Lord and Master.

Before she commenced to plan what answer to give to her parents and what steps to take, she knelt down in prayer to bring the burden, which was too heavy for her, to the Lord. When her communion with her Savior came to an end and she arose from her knees, the decision was made once for all. After this not even the thought entered into her heart to abandon her Redeemer for the sake of father, mother, or anyone else. Her future she committed to the Lord in believing prayer, and she felt certain that He never would leave her without His mercy and help. He has not called in vain to Himself all those who labor and are heavy laden.

For the last time Judith laid down her head on her own bed for the night in the home of her parents. A deep peace that passeth understanding filled her heart. She was now ready and willing if it had to be to leave her dear home forever.

Judith did not intend to remain in G——, not for one day. She knew it would be too hard to be so near to her dear ones, friends, and acquaintances. Therefore, she purposed to go to the city of M——. Then she would be far away from all former acquaintances. She knew that in M—— there was a large Christian church like the one in G—— where she had found the Lord. Besides, she hoped to find easier work to earn her living. After making these resolutions, Judith fell into a sweet, restful sleep.

In the morning, she met her parents at the breakfast table. With tears, she told them of her decision to remain faithful to her Lord and Savior even if she had to leave home for it.

"Papa," she said to her father, "you and Mama requested yesterday that I should make my choice between my Lord and you. I have prayed and meditated much over it, and I am willing if you demand it to leave the house . . . rather . . ." Tears made it impossible for her to say another word. Crying bitterly, she left the table, seeking refuge in her room.

"Nothing can be done! These people have corrupted Judith entirely," said Mr. Weinberg gloomily when Judith left the dining-room. "Let her go! It is utterly impossible to keep her in our house any longer."

"Yes, it is hopeless," added the mother. "Judith is lost for us. At times, however, I feel hopeful again that she might yet return. The other day I found out that she is not yet considered to be a member of the Christian church. I have learned that before they accept new members they baptize them by immersion in water first. Judith has not been baptized yet, as I was able to learn. This fact encourages me, as it gives me a faint hope of her coming back. Not all is lost yet. We have to do whatever we can to prevent her staying in this city. Her presence here would be an awful disgrace to us. And besides, being here near this church, she would very likely join it, and then of course it would be hopeless. The best would be if she would go to a distant place. The life far away from home might help to make her sober. Let her try to live independently."

At this moment Judith reëntered. She had sobbed out her grief and was now quiet. After taking her seat at the table, she turned to her parents: "I told you before that I was willing to leave home if you want me to. But I think it would be too hard for you and for me, too, should I remain in G———. Therefore, I thought it would be best for me to go to M———."

After a short silence, the father said: "Well, you may go. I shall try to get a ticket for you to M——— today, and you leave tomorrow with the morning train. Prepare her clothes and whatever else she needs for the trip," he said to his wife. "I have to attend to my business now."

He arose and left the house.

After packing her things, Judith found a few minutes to go and see some of her Christian friends. She wanted to say good-by and tell them about her leaving town. The Christians knew of the severe suffering of Judith, and many prayers ascended up to the throne of grace for her in their prayer-meetings as well as in their homes. They asked the Lord to help Judith to bear all hardships and persecutions and to keep her true and faithful and also to relieve her suffering. The news of her going away was therefore met by the members of the church with great joy, seeing in it a direct answer to her prayers. Departing now from her, they prayed the blessings of the Lord upon her and wished her well. The pastor of the church gave her a number of addresses of Christians and also a letter of introduction to the pastor of the church in M———, in which he asked the latter to accept Judith as a faithful child of God and to assist her in every way, as she was a stranger in M———.

The parting with her parents and sisters was very cool. They all looked upon her as an enemy. The mother and sisters did not even go with her to the depot. This cold, heartless treatment of her dear ones lay like a heavy stone upon her heart. But the Lord, for whose sake she was persecuted and despised, did not allow her to leave the city weighed down with sorrow and grief. He had prepared a fine surprise and joy for her.

As Judith arrived with her father at the depot, she was amazed to see all the members of the church gathered on the platform. The daughter of the minister, her former fellow-student, greeted her, presenting to her a beautiful bouquet of fresh flowers from the Christian young people's society. This farewell the Christians gave was touching indeed. Each had a verse for her or a word of cheer and comfort on the way. Only her father turned his back on her and talked to some Jews whom he met there.

The song of a wonderful Christian farewell hymn filled the place when the train started to move. The words were something like this: "The hour of separation has come. We have to depart now. The grief of our hearts is known only by God and ourself, etc." Many sang with tears in their eyes; all felt sorry to separate from Judith. All had learned to love her dearly, as a true child of God. The sorrow, however, was intermingled with joy as they thought of what suffering and persecutions Judith was now delivered from.

A mixed feeling of joy and deep pain filled Judith's heart as she stood at the open door of the car waving good-by with her handkerchief to her dear friends in Christ. She felt heartbroken that her father had not a word to say to her before she left. He seemed not even to notice that the train was carrying his daughter away. He did not even say good-by to her.

Persecuted for Christ's Sake

Gathering speed, the train moved swiftly away from the station. For a long time, Judith remained near the open door, looking back at the city in which she had experienced so much during the last years. Here she had fallen in love with Solomon and had been for a time so happy and cheerful. She had voluntarily given up this love for the love of her Redeemer and Lord, to Whom she had given her heart. In this city she had undergone the severest trials of her life, and here she had felt for the first time the hatred of dear ones and friends. The testing of her faith had been so hard that she would have broken down under the burden had not the Lord carried her through. Here the warmest bonds of love between her parents, the beloved sisters, her nation and herself had been loosed. She had given up all earthly things that had been dear to her in order to win the heavenly, immortal blessings.

Judith had reached this all, not without great inner struggles and self-denials. Only her great love to her Lord gave her courage and strength to go through and to continue in the way she had started. Now she was an exile, cast out from her own home and from her nation. At this thought, her heart was pressed anew with a severe pain, and big tear-drops ran down her pale cheeks. For the last time she looked back to the disappearing city, and a heavy sigh escaped her breast. "Good-by all, perhaps forever!" her lips uttered as she went to her compartment.

She was very glad to find that there were no other passengers besides herself, and she thanked the Lord for this time of quietness with Him alone.

"Now I have become a pilgrim and a stranger, like Abraham," thought the girl. "All my relatives and friends are left behind . . . Praise and thanks be to

Thee, my Savior, that Thou who didst not leave Abraham nor any other of Thy faithful children, art going with me, Thy weak and inexperienced child."

After this short prayer Judith began to sing softly her most beloved hymn, which she had delighted to sing in the meetings with the other Christians, as well as in her room in times when the waves of testing were going high:

Jesus, I my cross have taken,
All to leave and follow Thee;
Destitute, despised, forsaken,
Thou from hence my all shalt be.

CHORUS:
I will follow Thee, my Savior,
Thou didst shed Thy blood for me,
And though all the world forsake Thee,
By Thy grace I'll follow Thee.

Perish every fond ambition,
All I've sought, and hop'd, and known;
Yet how rich is my condition!
God and heaven are still my own.

Let the world despise and leave me;
They have left my Savior, too —
Human hearts and looks deceive me —
Thou art not, like them, untrue.

And whilst Thou shalt smile upon me,
God of wisdom, love, and might,
Foes may hate, and friends disown me:
Show Thy face and all is bright.

Man may trouble and distress me,
'Twill but drive me to Thy breast;
Life with trials hard may press me,
Heaven will bring me sweeter rest.

This song was the fervent prayer of her longing heart. And the Lord was with her, for He has promised to be with all who give their hearts to Him, until the end of the world. He, the Good Shepherd, took care of His lonely sheep, and she was always able under all circumstances to find rest on His bosom. She had learned in the days of sorrow and persecution to trust Him fully in everything. Her unknown future she also committed into His loving hands. She knew that the first friend to meet her in the strange city would be He Who had accompanied her all the way from G——, for God has pledged Himself to keep the going out and the coming in of His children here on earth.

Judith's trust in the Lord proved to be not in vain. He never left her. She had left home, parents, sisters, and her nation for His name's sake, and she received a hundredfold brothers and sisters. She had obtained also another nation, a people of God, not in name only, but who indeed belonged to Him and served Him wholeheartedly, a nation to which belong all those who have accepted the Lord Jesus Christ and are washed in His precious blood and set apart from every tribe and nation living here on earth.

Having several addresses of Christians in M—— and also a letter of introduction to the pastor of the Evangelical church there, Judith had gone from the depot to the home of the latter at her arrival in M——. The members of the church and especially the young people did all they could to assist Judith and to make her present condition as easy as possible. With their help, Judith soon found employment in an office of a city institution. Her heart was touched by the love she met through God's children in G—— and the new place, for which she praised the Lord. This love and care of the Christians strengthened her faith greatly and made her cleave closer to her Lord. Through it she came to love His people more, and she felt more attached to them each day.

Judith's life in M—— was greatly blessed of the Lord. He recompensed her for all she had suffered for Him previously. Earning her own living, she was independent and could serve her Lord unimpeded. And Judith did indeed serve. Before long she became a member of the young people's society. She sang in the choir. Being fond of children, she soon became a teacher in the Sunday school. Frequently she witnessed for her Lord in the meetings of the young people, at the place where she worked, and wherever there was an opportunity. Her oral testimony she made more effective through her life and deeds. Having grown up in the midst of plenty, surrounded by luxury, Judith had never been used to do any physical work and now she was especially eager to help those who were weak or unable to work. Together with a group of Christian girls, she visited the sick and poor in the homes, taking care of them when necessary, cleaning the rooms, and helping in whatever way she could. Helping the poor and needy was a source of great joy to her as well as to many others. Her humble eagerness to serve provoked many of the members of the young people's society to do likewise. Judith had brought with her a new supply of joy, vigor, and blessings into this society.

Spring came. Everything began to blossom and grow. The meadows and forests once more had put on their beautiful apparel, as if for a wedding, and they were filled with the merry song of the multitude of happy birds. Life had come forth after the long, cold death of winter. Judith loved the outdoors, and when going out on Sundays to the country with groups of the young people, she enjoyed every flower, the trees, and the grass. Her heart was filled with praise and worship to her Creator, Who had freed the earth from frost and ice and Who also had freed her heart from the bondage of darkness, sin, and death, and had quickened her soul to a new life. A wonderful spring of eternal life and glory had commenced in Judith's heart. The icy cover of sin and death had been removed forever.

"Life, life has come! Eternal life," sang a sweet voice in her heart. Judith had life indeed, and she had it abundantly, not only for herself, but she carried life to those who were still in spiritual death.

She liked to go on Sundays and holidays with other young people to the neighboring villages. There she read with great pleasure portions of the gospel, to those who gathered around her, mostly simple, illiterate people. These plain, ignorant country folk, who did not know much about Christ and His love, were dear to her. She felt sorry that they had been given the name of Christians but nobody had told them about their Savior Who had died on the cross to save them. She had never known before nor come into contact with the common Russian people, as she had always lived in a city, and there she had been associated only with the Jews. Being educated in a strictly Jewish spirit, she was taught to consider the Russians a heathen nation adverse to God, but since she came to know these people, she was willing to consecrate her whole life to serve them.

Recalling her discourse with her grandfather, who attempted to prove that the Lord Jesus Christ was not the Messiah of Israel by telling her of the life of the Greek Orthodox, the Roman Catholics, and other nominal Christians who lived around them, Judith understood now why these so-called Christians hated the Jews and why they strove and quarreled among themselves, having even religious and political wars. She realized now that the majority of these "Christians" bear the name of Christ unconsciously and that they are opposing Christ as did the Jews. She saw that these Christians as well as the Jews know neither Christ nor His gospel and therefore do not live a life of love one to another as Christ revealed to us. The one as well as the other were just as ignorant concerning Christ Jesus and His redemption as she had been for many years. Knowing this made her more zealous to tell the story wherever she could.

While her work was done mostly among the Russians, there was still a warm love in her heart for her own people, the children of Israel. Whenever she met with Jews, be it in her office, on the street, or whatever place it was, she redeemed the opportunity and spoke to them of her Savior, the Lord Jesus Christ. Usually she met with derision and enmity. It was different with these simple Russian country people. They liked to listen and were attentive when she read to them or told the gospel stories in simple words. She saw many times how one woman or the other quietly wiped their tears from their eyes.

In the young people's society, Judith was always the initiator and organizer of the visiting groups for evangelistic work in the country towns and villages. She waited impatiently for the days set for their visitation in the villages around M——.

One evening there was a special evangelistic meeting in the church, which was conducted by a missionary, a converted Jew. He gave a stirring message, and at the close of the meeting several arose and asked the church to accept them into membership. The courage of these young Christians awakened in Judith the same desire.

Repeatedly she had been thinking of joining the church. It was quite a while since she had given her heart to Jesus Christ, but she had not yet formally joined the church. She knew that the Christians loved her as a sister in the Lord but she knew also that all the members of the church had become such through baptism. Studying the Word of God, she had become convinced that she, too, had to fulfill the will of the Lord in this. But until this day she had lacked courage to take this last decisive step. Two things had prevented her from becoming a member of the church. First, she thought she was not yet enough established in her faith, and she feared that she might stumble on her way and, belonging to a church, she might through it provoke the sneers of the unbelievers and the church would be dishonored because of her; second, the great love for her dear mother.

She knew too well that as soon as she would be baptized and join the church formally all relations between her and home would be severed forever; she was still corresponding with her dear ones.

Seeing the determination of these fellow-Christians and being convinced that the Lord wanted her to join she decided to do it. It was much harder for Judith to decide than it was for those of the Gentiles, for baptism was going to separate her from her nation and their religion. The inner separation had taken place long before, and now she was going to do it formally and publicly.

Rising to her feet, Judith made her desire known to the church. The Christians met her application with great joy and gratitude to the Lord. Thus Judith severed the last connections with the past and gave herself fully to the new life she had found in the Lord Jesus Christ. She was determined to follow Him without looking back.

A year had passed since Judith left her home and went to M———. Now and then she had received letters from her mother and sisters. Each letter had brought new exhortations and pleas from her mother to come back to the faith of her fathers, to her nation, and to the home of her parents. Judith shed many tears when reading these letters. She prayed daily, earnestly to the Lord for conversion of her dear ones. Their letters, however, revealed how far their hearts were away from Him.

Her father had come twice to M——— for business. He had stopped to see Judith. But these visits were very brief. He was always cool and stern. Mr. Weinberg was careful never to ask about or to speak of her convictions. He usually asked coolly about her health and a few unimportant questions about her life, delivered the greetings of mother and sisters and left, giving some slight excuse for his haste.

In the last letters, Judith's mother had been more insistent than ever upon her coming home. Judith, too, had a great longing to see her dear mother and sisters once more though she now dreaded the meeting with them, especially with her mother, for she had been told that her father while in M—— had gathered information about her life and activity and of her attitude toward Christianity from the Jews of the city. Probably her mother did not yet know of her baptism and her joining the Christian church but doubtless she would ask her about that should she come home, and the thought of the consequence frightened Judith.

Nevertheless Judith yielded to the persistent pleas of her mother and the impulse of her own heart and went home when a month's vacation was given her. A mixed feeling of joy and dull apprehension made her heart beat faster as she approached the house of her parents. The mother and her sisters met her with great joy and love. They had been waiting impatiently for her arrival. Having always lived in close friendship together, and being devoted one to another, they had missed Judith very much after her departure. Besides, the mother was cherishing the hope that Judith after the hard experience of being far away from home and providing for her own living would have become discouraged and weak and would now easily yield to their petitions to come back to their religion.

A few pleasant days were spent joyfully together in the home. The two younger sisters were eager to tell Judith all that had happened in her absence in the city. Ruth had finished college and was preparing to enter university in the fall to study medicine. She liked to talk with Judith about it and to make plans.

"Would it not be lovely," she said almost daily, "if you remain in M—— and I could study there? Then we could live together in one room. I should be so glad."

Judith had to tell her sisters many things of interest, too. But she as well as Ruth and Sara were careful to avoid the question of her religious convictions. The mother, though somewhat remote, was kind and good to Judith. But she as well as her younger daughters was all the time inwardly disturbed about the burning question of Judith's religion. In her letters, Judith had never mentioned anything about not wanting to provoke her mother more than necessary.

This delicate question, however, solved itself on the first Sunday of Judith's stay at home. On this day the stores of Mr. Weinberg were closed according to the laws of the country, and the whole family decided to go to the theater. Nobody asked Judith beforehand if she was going or not. When the time came and the others began to dress, she said that she would rather stay at home. Her father turned and made a grimace but said nothing, while her mother flushed with sore displeasure as she looked in surprise at Judith. This refusal to visit the theater was to them most eloquent testimony of her standing. They all saw that the desired change for which they had so hoped had not taken place. Judith had remained true to her accepted principles. From this evening the relation between Judith and her parents changed greatly. They became cool and distant.

About three days later, Ruth and Sara went to see Judith in her room after they had finished their duties of the day. They had been talking about her during the day and were determined to go to Judith herself and ask her for the reason for her refusal to accompany them on Sunday. Then they thought they would use the opportunity and persuade her to leave her silly convictions, as the two called it between themselves.

Judith had been praying all the time for her sisters, and since she had come home, she was asking God for a special opportunity to speak to them of the Lord Jesus Christ. She was afraid to start a conversation of this kind with them, knowing that her sisters had been prejudiced by others against her and they would never listen to her should she begin to speak about their souls.

Now, Judith was exceedingly happy to see her dear sisters come into her room, and she believed that this was the God-sent chance. Seating them one on each side of her on the sofa, she listened to what they had to ask and to tell her. After they had finished, she began to explain to them with great love and tenderness why she had refused to go with them to the theater and that her faith in Christ was not a silly caprice or delusion but a deeply and seriously considered obedience to the will of God.

Taking from the little table her beloved Bible, with which she now never parted, Judith commenced to read to her sisters one after another promise of God to Israel concerning the Messiah. She read also how the Messiah came to our earth in the person of Jesus of Nazareth and how the Jews rejected their Messiah, crying: "We will not that this man reign over us," and then they crucified Him, nailing Him to the Cross of Calvary.

Judith opened her heart to the two girls, telling them how she had been occupied with questions about God since she was a little girl. She mentioned how she once had overheard a discussion of her grandfather and two other rabbis about "Yeshua," and how one of the rabbis had proved to the others that "Yeshua" was indeed the Messiah of Israel. At this she was looking with her merry eyes at Ruth, asking her if she did not remember how she woke up one night and saw her sitting on the window-sill while visiting Grandpa. Ruth was so absorbed in what Judith had told them that she only nodded her head silently.

"After this," continued Judith, "the thought of the Messiah and the question of who was this 'Yeshua' never left me entirely. Sometimes I forgot it for a while, but soon it came again. Then I commenced to read our Hebrew Bible carefully. The more I read, the more I became convinced in my heart that Jesus Christ was truly the Messiah of Israel. His earthly life is pictured especially clear and truthful in the fifty-third chapter of the prophet Isaiah. Here it is . . ."

Judith had opened her Bible, and she read the whole chapter.

"Being convinced that He is the Messiah, I did, however, know very little of Him and His life. I knew only what Grandpa had told me once about His suffering and death. I suppose you, too, still remember the story he told me one evening while sitting on the porch. Of course he assured me that 'Yeshua' was a deceiver and had died for His own guilt. However, the Lord for whom I had been searching and for whom my soul was longing, led me, as you know, to a Christian meeting. There I heard for the first time the truth about the Lord Jesus Christ. There I saw and became fully persuaded that He is the true Messiah of Israel, the Son of the Blessed, and my personal Savior. And since that evening, my heart belongs wholly to Him. The aim of my life is now to witness for Him, telling of His great love to poor sinners, that someone else of those who know nothing of Him and who hate and persecute Him may come to know Him also and become happy in Him.

"O my dear Ruth and Sara, how I do wish that you, too, might give Him your hearts. I am praying unceasingly to my Savior that this sooner or later might happen."

Judith's eyes began to fill with tears. She put her arms around both girls and, embracing, she kissed them warmly.

"It is such an unspeakable grief and pain to me to know that deep hidden in your heart there is hatred toward me. The only thing that comforts me is that you do it unknowingly. It has been instilled in you that I am an apostate, having abandoned God, an heretic who should in accordance with the law be stoned mercilessly. Today is the first chance that I could open my heart to you . . . I do not know how you will accept my words; that is up to you. You are no more children, and you are able to judge for yourselves. But I have one petition to you. Don't be too harsh with me, please. . . . Start to read this wonderful, holy Book, and the Lord will reveal Himself to you . . ."

"Please forgive me, Judith dear!" interrupted Ruth, tears flowing down her cheeks as she threw her arms around Judith's neck.

"Forgive me, too, please," said Sara, weeping bitterly.

For a few moments the three sisters were sitting silently embracing each other. It was very quiet. Only their sobs broke the stillness in the room.

"Why have we separated one from another?" sobbed Sara, leaning closer to Judith. "How cruel are people to sow dissension and hatred among us!"

"Our dear Judith, we did not know anything of what you have told us tonight. We two have never been interested in questions of religion or God. But one thing I do know now," said Ruth, determinedly, whatever may happen — I shall never cease to love you dearly with my whole heart. If there was anything in my heart against you, I ask you once more, please forgive me, dear Judith. May your God help and bless you!"

It was about one o'clock in the morning when Judith's sisters left her and went each to her room. They had left fully reconciled to their sister and with the firm determination to defend Judith wherever it would be necessary from the attacks of other people.

Being alone again, Judith lifted up her heart in fervent prayer to the Lord, praising Him for giving her this marvelous opportunity to speak to her sisters of Him. He had answered her prayers and given her what she had been asking and longing for. It made her very happy to know that her sisters loved her again and no longer hated her and that they now would be friends as they had been before.

"Oh, how merciful art Thou, and Thy loving kindness is marvelous, my blessed Redeemer! Thou hast always protected me under the shadow of Thy wings and hast helped me in my weakness. Please save my parents and sisters, too, and let them become Thy true disciples. Reveal Thyself in Thy love and glory to them as Thou hast done to me. Let them look upon Thee whom they have pierced. Praise, honor, and glory be to Thee for all Thou hast done for me, my Lord and my God." This was the earnest prayer of Judith before she retired for the night.

Two uneventful days had passed. Mother Weinberg and Ruth were sitting in the parlor. The other members of the family were not at home. Judith had gone to the prayer-meeting of the Christians. The two who had remained at home were engaged in a very serious conversation.

"Don't you want to follow in the footsteps of your precious sister?" asked the mother scornfully after a short, heavy pause, looking at her daughter with angry eyes.

"No, Mama," replied Ruth meekly, "but it seems to me it is very unjust and inhuman to treat Judith the way we all have done until the present for the only reason that she believes a little differently in God from the way we do."

"That isn't true! She has turned away from God and believes in a deceiver," retorted her mother sharply, being greatly provoked by her daughter's words.

"No, dear Mother, in the eyes of Judith 'Yeshua' is not a deceiver but the Messiah of the Jews. She is deeply convinced that this is true. But in case she is wrong, let God punish her for it. Why should we so mercilessly persecute her? And to be honest, has she changed to the worse since the day she became a Christian? I know it is contrariwise — she has become better. She is indeed an angel. We all hate and persecute her and she bears it meekly, forgives us, and continues to love us warmly and tenderly."

This was too much for the aggravated mother. She was so excited that she could not constrain herself any longer. Looking fiercely at the girl, she cried at the top of her voice: "What in the world has happened to you? Yesterday I heard the same story from Sara, and today you come with it, as if you had agreed to do so. Has this heretic succeeded already to pervert you, too, from the right way? Oh, why, why did I let her come home into my house?"

"Judith has not perverted us. About two or three days ago, Sara and I had a little talk with Judith, and we saw that there is no reason at all why we should hate our sister, but vice versa — we all ought to love her sincerely, for she loves us dearly."

"O Adonai — God! She has now corrupted these two also!" lamented the mother with flowing tears. "Why have I done it? . . . Why have I permitted her to come into my house? . . . O Ruth, is it possible that you did listen to her? And you believed what she told you? . . . That's why Sara spoke of her yesterday the way she did, and that's why you both seek to defend and justify her."

"Good evening," greeted Mr. Weinberg entering. "What are you talking about so loudly? What's the matter with you, Rachel?" He turned to his wife. "You seem to be so excited and upset. What has happened here?"

Ruth was pale and frightened. She was terrified by the result of her talk with her mother and the unexpected appearance of her father at this unpleasant moment. She had hoped to be able to reason with her mother but had failed.

After their talk with Judith both girls had made the decision in their hearts to speak to their mother about Judith but they failed to tell each other of their intention. So being desirous to help Judith, they had unwittingly called forth this awful storm in the heart of their mother. It pained Ruth very much to see that she had only harmed Judith through this intercourse. She felt crushed and sat very quietly with her head bowed.

"What is wrong with me?", sobbed Mrs. Weinberg. "Our whole family is perishing! What have I done? . . . Oh, what have I done?"

"Well, what has happened?" Mr. Weinberg was beginning to lose his patience.

"O David! There is a curse hovering over our house. Just think, this apostate has used the time that she is here to sow the seed of heresy in the hearts of her sisters. Yesterday it was Sara, and today Ruth comes to me and tries to vindicate her before me. I found out that she has managed to speak to them. I had hoped all the time that going through hardships and separation would make her sober and bring her to her senses and that she would repent and confess that she had gone astray, but all is in vain. We must find out once for all from her if she is willing to give up this heresy or not. I am going to ask her."

"I warned you in advance, Rachel, that you should not take her into our home. I suspect that she has already become a member of the Christian church. I tried to find out a few things from our Jews when I was in M—— the last time. They told me that she is active in the church there, having a part in everything, and I suppose that this would be possible only for members . . . Well, you now have to bear the consequence of your stubborn will. You have invited her, and now you may see to it how to straighten things out and how to get rid of her. I am sick and tired of it. As far as I am concerned, I look at her as a stranger, for our Judith is dead to me — she has died long ago."

"David, is it possible that our Judith has joined the Christians for good? . . . Is all lost and all hopes in vain?"

"I do not know," said her husband, shrugging his shoulders. "I have only expressed my opinions and suspicions, but let us leave it now and ask her later about it. Now, tell me what do you blame Ruth and Sara for? What have you to say about the things Mother was telling me?" inquired the father, turning to Ruth.

Lifting her head with a sigh and looking at her father, Ruth replied: "I do not know what to say, Daddy. I know one thing, that Judith has not corrupted us. The other day we went to her room, Sara and I, and we had a little talk with her, and we found out that there is not the slightest reason why we should hate her. Therefore, we thought we would speak to Mama about it. This is all I know and can tell you."

"You are right on the one hand, my girl," agreed her father. "Judith has not done any harm to us for which we ought to hate her. On the other hand, she has done very much against the religion of our fathers and against our honorable line of ancestors who have been the bearers of the religion Jehovah gave us for many centuries. How many stalwart warriors for the faith has our notable family produced in times past! And in the line of such a family there has come now an apostate who has abandoned the religion for which her ancestors were ready to shed the last drop of their blood. She is a disgrace to our family. How can we continue to love Judith? Our religion demands that we should stone such an one as she. We must hate every *Goyim*, but if some one of our people becomes a *Goyim*, we must not only hate him but it is our duty to exterminate him or her entirely. It is true the laws of the land we are now living in do not permit us to stone her, but nobody will hinder us in doing away with her from our home and from our society, and it is our holy duty to do it. We must not have anything to do with Judith in the future. I met our honorable rabbi the other day. He had heard of her being at home and so he asked me about her religious convictions. He wanted to know why we had taken her into our home. I told him, of course, that I did not know anything definite about her standing. However, if she still sticks to her heresy and even tries to entice others into it, then of course we have to get her out of our midst without hesitation. And we have to do this soon. By the way, where is Judith? Let her come and give a clear answer at once." The last words he spoke to his wife.

"Where she is? . . . Most likely with her dear friends, the *Goyim*," scoffed the latter. "Her nation and her family are nothing to her."

It was almost twelve o'clock when Judith returned home from the meeting. There she had found comfort and joy in the fellowship of God's children. She told them of her life and of the many blessings and marvelous help of the Lord she had experienced since she left G——. She mentioned also the glad fact that she had been baptized and accepted as a member in the church. The whole assembly joined in fervent prayer before the Lord, praising and worshipping Him for all He had done for Judith and asking Him to lead and guide her in the future as He had in the past.

Judith's parents agreed not to wait for her late that evening but have her give a final explanation on the next day. This she did. This was the last discourse with her parents. She never saw them again. May God grant them a meeting there beyond the river.

The next evening, Mr. Weinberg finished his business earlier than usual and went straight home. Soon the family gathered around the supper table. The atmosphere was charged, and no conversation was started. The parents were serious and gloomy, especially the mother, who was extremely nervous. During the whole day, she had avoided meeting Judith. The two younger girls were sad and depressed. The thought of the failure of their good intention oppressed them. Then they knew that an awful time was awaiting Judith after supper when the parents were going to demand an explanation and a final answer. They feared the outcome.

Judith had felt restless from the very morning. Her heart had been aching from an unknown grief. Though she knew nothing of what had happened the previous night, neither what was in store for her at the end of the day, she had felt miserable all day long. At the table, she was quiet and her little face looked very sober. The expression of the faces of the rest of the family caused her to suspect that something was wrong. Her heart quivered involuntarily.

The meal over, the younger girls were asked to occupy themselves with clearing the table. Looking sternly for a minute at Judith, her father asked her to come with her mother into his room. Upon entering, he closed the door carefully behind him and told Judith to take a seat opposite his chair. After a moment of ominous stillness, he turned to her.

"For a long while we have tried to help you to come back to the faith of our fathers, Judith, but with no effect. The last definite measure we tried was sending you away from home. Your mother hoped that this would make you sober and dispel your delusions. Now you have come home for a time into our house. We wanted to see you. Your mother and sisters could bear the separation no longer. Mother never gave up the hope that you finally would come back into our midst again. However, we have deceived ourselves, for instead of repenting and confessing your guilt, you begin to influence your sisters perniciously. Now is your last chance. We are asking you for the last time, will you return to us, to God, and to your nation? Or, better, is it still possible for you to be restored? Or have you joined their church already? I know they baptize first before they accept anyone. Have you been baptized? We, your parents, have to know these things. You must be honest and open and tell us the whole truth. We are here to hear you tonight."

The pause that followed was one never to be forgotten. Mrs. Weinberg was trembling with excitement. She held her husband's hand tightly in hers. Judith's eyes were lifted upward from whence she expected help for the crucial moment. In a short, silent prayer she sent up her cry to the Lord. Finally she turned her face full to her parents and began with a soft but firm voice: "Return to the God of my fathers? Dear Papa and Mama, I have turned to Him long ago. I believe in Him and serve Him the best I know."

A dark cloud of displeasure and scorn twisted the face of David Weinberg, but he held his peace, not wanting to interrupt his daughter.

"Concerning my sisters, I have never attempted to turn them away from God or to lead them into a heresy. I only told them that my desire is to serve my Lord all the days of my life and that it is inexpressibly hard for me that because of it I am hated and despised by those whom I love most. The people to whose church I belong are neither heathen nor *Goyim,* as they are being called. But they are true worshipers and servants of the blessed Jehovah, Who came and took upon Himself the form of men and died as the guiltless Lamb of God for the sin of Israel and for the iniquity of the whole world. Concerning baptism — I can only say that I am now willing to do His will everywhere in everything. And He has said: 'He that believeth and is baptized shall be saved; but he that believeth not shall be condemned!' Being His handmaiden, I obey Him, and so I have done according to His holy commandment. I believe that He is the Son of God and my Savior; therefore I was baptized in His name."

"O Adonai — God!" exclaimed the mother, nervously wringing her hands. "Oh, what must I hear from my own child! Why have I given you birth?" Suddenly,

"I shall strangle you this very minute with my own hands!"

With this, the furious mother made a mad rush toward Judith. Her face was pale and ugly with rage. Mr. Weinberg was immediately at her side. Seizing both her hands, he stood between mother and daughter.

"Be cursed! I am cursing you with the curse of a mother, and I shall not rest until I see you dead at my feet!" A heart-rending shriek pierced the air, and she was unconscious on the floor.

Judith, though numb and heartbroken, threw herself toward her mother, but before she was able to touch her, she was roughly stopped by her father. His voice was hoarse and hissing as he, pushing her aside and pointing at the door, roared at her: "Get out! Don't you dare touch her! You have no right to go near her! Get out! Do not dare to come under our eyes anymore! There is no longer room for you in our house!"

He lifted his wife up and put her on the couch. Then he walked to the door, opened it wide, and drove out his daughter, who was still standing on the same spot benumbed, her face pale and her eyes open in anguish.

Almost unconscious, as in a delirium, Judith reached her room and fell prostrate upon her bed. The terrible looking countenance of her mother was haunting her, and the shocking words of her curse still sounded in her ears.

Suddenly the door opened and, as Judith lifted up her eyes, she saw Ruth and Sara at the threshold, both crying. Judith arose and sat down at the edge of the bed. The girls at the door looked very much distressed, and finally Ruth sobbed between the tears: "Father sent us to tell you to leave our house immediately. He does not want Mother to see you anymore."

"Leave the house?" repeated Judith, bewildered. "Oh, yes, I am cursed! My own dear mother has cursed me," she said this slowly as if to herself. "Have I to leave right away?"

"Yes, Father demands it," stammered her sisters.

"O my God, do not leave me now!" breathed Judith in the anguish of her heart. "Strengthen me, O Lord! I do not know what to do. . . . Must leave . . . I am cursed . . ." whispered her deathly pale lips.

"Oh, you are waiting for me to leave, are you?" turned Judith to her sisters, who were still standing motionless at the threshold watching her.

"Well, I shall go," Judith arose quickly and dressed. Of all her things in the room, she took only her beloved Bible from the table. She approached her sisters to kiss them good-by, but both drew back as she came nearer.

"I forgot that I am cursed. You cannot touch me! Good-by then! The Lord bless Papa, Mama, and you both. . . ."

Judith staggered toward the front door as in a dream. The sobbing of Ruth and Sara made her turn and look at them once more. It was for the last time. Then she was on the street.

It was a cold night in the early spring. The snow had begun to melt during the day, but at night there was still frost. A cold breeze blew into Judith's face. For a few minutes she stood there near the door as if paralyzed. At last she turned and walked slowly down

Persecuted for Christ's Sake

the street. The streets were brightly lighted, and crowds of people were walking up and down chatting merrily. Among these were a large number of young Jews, old friends and acquaintances. They all knew that Judith was home on a visit, but they all despised her. Not one of them greeted her or spoke a word to her as she passed them now. They turned away as if they did not even notice her.

Passing through the lighted streets of the central part of the city, Judith was coming to the poorer section of the outskirts, which was dark and deserted. Suddenly she stopped abruptly as if awakening from a sleep. The silence of the night surrounded her. The working people who lived here had retired for the night. All was dark except the little lights that stole timidly through a few windows.

"What has happened to me? Where am I going?" she asked, in a low voice. Like a flash came the whole tragic evening before her again.

"They have damned and cursed me and driven me out!"

Judith lifted her eyes full of tears to the sky with its multitude of twinkling and sparkling stars.

"Thou seest me from the heights of Thy throne, my Lord. Take me, Thy weak and lonely child, by Thy hand and help me in this dark moment. Thou knowest that I am all alone in this world! Abide Thou with me!"

This short communion with the Lord under the canopy of the starry sky had a quieting effect upon her so that she was now able to think calmly.

"It's night and there will be no train until the morning. Besides, I have neither money nor anything else.

All I have has remained at home, from which I am banished. I can never go back to it again. The best I can do under present circumstances is to go to the home of the pastor. My Lord will not leave me. He will show me the next step I shall take," was the conclusion to which Judith came.

The pastor himself opened the door at her knock. Great was his surprise to see Judith before him at such a late hour of the night. She passed him silently, and without waiting for an invitation to take a seat she fell on the chair near the wall, breaking down under the terrific strain of the battle she had been fighting during the last hours in her heart. Judith had always been careful not to let others see the tears she shed under the burden of suffering and persecution, but now her grief was too great. She was unable to hide it and to bear it alone. An uncontrollable sobbing shook her whole frame convulsively.

The minister, his wife, and his daughter were sitting silently for a long time looking with tears of warm sympathy upon the heartbroken girl. They felt that something very serious had happened to Judith, for they knew how courageously and bravely she had borne all former trials. No one had ever seen her weeping and complaining. Her unexpected and late appearance, too, told a tale of crucial experience.

When the first severe spell was over and Judith had become a little more quiet, she felt a pair of tender, loving arms around her neck. She lifted her heavy, swollen eyes. There was Elizabeth, her schoolmate, close by. She was the girl from whom Judith had seen for the first time the light of the gospel truth. Elizabeth was looking at her with her beautiful, soothing, deep blue eyes, which were filled with tears of loving sympathy.

"Peace be unto thee, my dear Judith," she said softly, kissing her friend heartily. The girls who through the blood and the love of Jesus Christ were made sisters in Him, stood for a few minutes silently embracing each other. After Judith had recovered and gained sufficient quietness, she told her friends what she had gone through in the last few hours.

Taking his New Testament from the table, the servant of God began to read about the suffering and death of the Lord Jesus Christ, beginning at His triumphant entry into Jerusalem.

"Dear sister," he said to Judith after finishing the reading, "see what our Creator had to endure from His own creation. When thèy whom He had made crucified Him, He prayed for His tormentors, saying, 'Father, forgive them, for they know not what they do.' We are His disciples, and we have to go the same way toward our great goal. On this our way we, too, have to pass Gethsemane and Calvary. Today you have reached Gethsemane. Your soul is sorrowing even unto death. But be not fearful. He will strengthen and uphold you. Perhaps you will have to go over Golgotha, too, in the future. He will be there with you. He never forsakes His own. He has gone this way before us. Let us never take our eyes from Him Who has gone ahead of us and Who has loved us unto death, even unto death on the cross. We will follow His noble and holy example in this hour. May not grief overpower our hearts that we should fall asleep because of our sorrow, as did the disciples in Gethsemane. Let us pray now, and He will be with us and help us to bear it all victoriously."

Sincere and fervent prayers went up from the oppressed hearts to the throne of grace. Greatly strengthened by the Lord and the sympathetic prayers of His saints, Judith felt comforted. The seal of peace was again upon her attractive countenance, which seemed to be transfigured by the presence of Christ.

The next morning Judith took the train to M———. The Christians had kindly supplied her with money and the most necessary things for the trip. Many wishes of blessing accompanied her. This was the last morning she ever spent in this city. She was moving away speedily from the place where her dearly beloved parents, her sisters, Solomon, and the dear congregation of God were left behind. She was leaving the place, never to see it again, where she first met her Savior, and where she gave her young heart to Him, where she had stood the hardest test in her life and had remained faithful and loyal to her God. Indeed, this city had been Gethsemane to her, and she had come forth victoriously.

Once more the scene at the depot passed before her. Many of the Christian friends had been there, and she had been touched to see the many tears of love and sympathy. She still heard them say, "Good-by, Judith, dear! Good-by our dear sister in the Lord! Shall we ever see you here on earth again? Or perhaps it will be only there, at home, when we are with the Lord forever."

V

DEDICATED TO THE LORD

Meeting the Missionary — Decision to Devote Her Life for Service — The Work and Its Hardships — Illness

THERE HAD BEEN a blessed revival in the Evangelical church of M———. It was about a week since an evangelist from another part of Russia had arrived. Through his stirring messages, full of love and inspiration, the Holy Spirit touched the hearts of the roughest and hardest sinners and awakened them to a new life in Christ Jesus. Many repented and found forgiveness and peace. The Christians were stirred up to a new love and more zeal to work for the Lord, to be used of Him to bring those into the fold who were yet dead in sin and far away from the Shepherd. These days were for a large number days of cleansing and sanctification. On the last evening before his departure, the evangelist gave a message exclusively for the Christians.

"Open your eyes and look around you," he said at the close. "For several years our whole country has been saturated with brother-blood. Every day carries thousands of unsaved souls into a Christless grave and into eternal suffering.

"Our land is like an erupting volcano or a raging sea, whose billows rush and roar like a hungry tiger and nothing can calm them. Look and see the multitudes of seafarers perishing in the waves. Listen to the desperate calls for help that come to us from this sea of humanity. The S.O.S. comes from every city, every village, and home from the shores of the Arctic Sea to the burning Colchis.* Who will stretch out a brotherly hand to the perishing ones? Who will hear and respond to their cry? Is nobody there? It seems everybody is armed today against everybody else.

"Should not we Christians follow the example of our Lord and Master today? Should we not forget ourselves and plunge into the threatening elements of human vengeance and strife to save immortal souls from the grip of sin and Satan even if it be at the cost of our own lives?

"The life of our blessed Lord and Savior was the most precious life not only on earth but in the whole universe, and He laid it down for our salvation. Should we then think our lives too precious? Should we not willingly give them for the salvation of others? It is true that those of you in advanced age cannot go out and meet the privations and hardships, neither those who have families. The duty of such is to help with their prayers and to see to it that their children are brought up in the fear and knowledge of God and that they have their daily bread. But how about you, my young brethren and sisters? You are young and full of life and energy. There is no obstacle in your way. You are free. Souls are perishing, going into eternal condemnation! The Lord is calling! Who will go? 'Whom shall I send?' saith the Lord.

"Tonight He is speaking to you through me. Who would be willing to join us, a little group, and go from

* Transcaucasia

city to city, from village to village, from house to house, to preach the gospel and seek the lost? Of course this work is not for the cowardly and fainthearted. It demands courage and endurance, for we meet on our way hunger, exhaustion from the long journeys on foot, persecution and perhaps even death. Having experienced a great deal of hardship myself, I know what it means and, therefore, I warn all those who might think or desire to go out into the field that you may give it very earnest consideration and prayer first. Don't start out and then retreat after the first attempt. But to all who have a firm, strong heart, the Lord has a word to say: 'Be faithful unto death, and I will give you the crown of life!' Now, then — who is willing? Who will go?"

The last call died slowly among the crowded pews. A solemn stillness reigned. The minister of Christ watched the audience prayerfully.

Many hearts present belonged to the Lord. A goodly number were active church-members who were eager to glorify their Master. But to respond to an appeal such as this seemed too hard for many. The terrible fire of the civil war had been raging in the land for years. In many places famine was rampant. Various epidemic diseases, the inevitable result of war and famine, were taking the lives of thousands. So the lives and possessions of the people were made very insecure by soldiers and diseases. Nobody felt safe in his own home. Going in such a time from place to place preaching the gospel was far more dangerous. The audience of this unselfish and devoted servant of Christ realized this fact.

"I am willing to answer the call of my Lord!" said a quiet but steady voice from one of the back seats.

At once all turned around to see who it was who had thus responded to the appeal. It was a girl young in years and frail in body with big, pretty, thoughtful dark eyes.

"I am dedicating my life wholly to Him. Though I am not strong and not fit for such work, I know that He is able to work through me. I am inexperienced in the Lord's work, but I do love Him and those for whom He gave His life."

"Judith!" went the whisper all over the church.

Yes, it was Judith. On her return to M—— after the painful parting from home and parents, Judith continued to work for her living. But every spare minute she devoted to her service of love. Her greatest pleasure was to visit the sick and take care of them. She comforted the sorrowing and helped the needy around her. On Sundays and holidays she went as before to the villages, where she spread joy and light by telling the simple story of salvation and helping the people in their spiritual and bodily needs.

Although this was a blessed ministry, Judith had been longing for a larger possibility and for full-time service. After she had come to know the plain, unlearned Russian country people who knew little about the blessed Savior of men though they were named after His name, she had embraced them heartily with her rich love. Several times the thought had come to her to give up her employment, which limited her, and trust the Lord for the supplying of all her needs and go to this people to live with them and to lead them to Christ. But she had put it off so far because she was not sure if the Lord wanted her to do it and if such kind of service would be pleasing to Him. As she now

Dedicated to the Lord

heard this man of God plead for workers, she had the assurance that the moment had come when the desire of her heart was going to be fulfilled.

Judith had attended every meeting of the evangelist as his faithful helper. She prayed for him while he gave the message and in the inquiry room she was always busy speaking to and praying with seeking souls. His inspiring sermons had kindled in her heart a warmer love for the lost and a greater zeal for service in God's vineyard.

She did not waver a minute when she heard of the need for workers. An encouraging voice was saying to her, "Now is the time. This is your way, Judith. The longings of your soul will now be realized." Therefore she arose and said, "I am ready." And she was ready, indeed. God Himself had prepared His instrument to His honor and glory.

At the close of the meeting, she consulted the evangelist about the details, and he gave her the address and time to join the other missionaries. Judith was very happy and contented that the Lord had led and guided her so marvelously. She was not blinded by illusions. She knew that the way she had chosen was not an easy one. It would mean self-denial and hardships, but it did not frighten her. She felt deep in her heart an unsurpassed peace and joy. The blessed assurance that the Lord was going with her was very precious. It was His way, and she was willing to follow His footsteps.

The day of her departure came. Many of her Christian friends went to the station to see her off. One of the girls who had worked more with Judith than the others, asked with tears: "My dear Judith, are you leaving us for long? For what length of time have you joined this mission?"

"I think, dear Jean, that I have dedicated myself for lifetime to the Lord and His work," replied Judith, looking thoughtfully into the distance. "That's my desire, at least."

The work Judith was entering into was indeed very hard. The warning of the evangelist had not been exaggerated. Each day brought new trials and privations. Some days the hardships were more than she had expected. Such life was severe, especially for Judith. Her health was not good and she was not used to being taxed so hard, as she had lived all her life under the constant care of loving, circumspect, and wealthy parents. Those around her were often forced to think that she would not be able to continue her work much longer. But the love and compassion for the suffering ones inspired her every day anew. Not having strength of her own, she was leaning hard upon Him Who was able to supply all she needed moment by moment.

The ocean of misery and distress on every side demanded ever increasing self-sacrifice and untiring labor. A great spiritual hunger was evident everywhere. Men and women, and even young children, were tired and weary from strife, war, and the daily fear of death. They were longing and thirsting for peace and rest in Christ. Many accepted the gospel that was preached to them with great eagerness and gratitude to the Lord. In every place where the missionaries brought the tidings of peace, sinners broke down under the burden of sin and found forgiveness, peace, and life eternal. Besides spiritual famine, the mission

Dedicated to the Lord

workers met in every village much physical poverty and diseases. These unfortunate people were all left without any medical help and proper care (doctors and druggists had fled to save their lives) and they died by the scores, often whole families. There were cases where one member after the other died, and the dead were in the houses sometimes for weeks before somebody happened to enter. Together with the others, Judith gave herself whole-heartedly to the task of helping these sufferers, not sparing her own health and strength in the effort to make their lot a little easier.

So the life of Judith was spent day after day. The Lord had given her this field of labor, and she accomplished her part in it with great joy and gratitude to the Master.

It was an unusually warm summer. The air was hot, as though heated, and one could breathe only with difficulty. The heavy, biting dust from the street filled the rooms of the small cottages in the village in which there were many sick ones. There was no escape from the heat and the dust.

Several days previously a group of strangers had come to a village in southern Russia and were lodging in one of the houses of its outskirts that was pleasantly located in the midst of an orchard. Three of these strangers had contracted typhus and were very ill — nearer to death than to life. Two others were taking turns in caring for the sick ones day and night.

It was one of the hot summer nights. The air was sultry and suffocating. It was extremely hard for the patients, who were hardly able to breathe. All windows were wide open, but no breeze found its way in.

Near the one window that opened into the orchard, stood a bed on which lay a young girl. For several hours she had been in a delirium. At the table near by sat "Grandpa" Asin. (So the leader of the party was called by those who labored with him.) He was attentively watching the patient before him who was staring at him while pointing into the distance with her thin white hand and speaking very rapidly.

As the patient seemed to address him, "Grandpa" Asin leaned over, eager to catch her words. Disappointed, he shook his head. He could not understand a word, for the girl was speaking in the old Hebrew language. Suddenly she regained consciousness and, stretching out her weak, trembling hand to her friend, she asked, "Didn't you understand me, Grandpa? I thought that you understood all I said."

Her friend took her hand into his and feeling her pulse, he answered, "No, I could not understand a word. Who was with you? What disturbed you so, Judith? You spoke for nearly two hours and were excited all the time."

"Oh, I saw such a wonderful vision, Grandpa. You and I were somewhere in a gorgeous temple that was crowded to the limit with Jews. The high priest was there, too, in his beautiful, sumptuous priestly robe. In the middle of the temple was a poorly clad man. He stood there silently. His eyes were turned toward the eastern part of the building where they rested upon the multitude of people. I could not take my eyes from Him. Somehow I felt that this must be the Lord Jesus Christ, the Messiah of Israel, Who had come now to His people. You told me, too, that this was He . . . I decided then that I would testify before this multitude

Dedicated to the Lord

that He had saved me from my sins and that He was willing and able to save everyone.

"I began to tell them what Christ had done for me. He remained all the while in the same place. I pointed to Him, telling them that He was there in our midst, but evidently for some reason they could not see Him. Nevertheless, many who heard my words commenced to cry and to smite their breasts. Many of the people and even the high priest threw up their hands and cried for forgiveness, weeping and wailing. I was so happy over their reptentance, but I had to strain my voice much so they could hear me in spite of the great commotion and noise. That was very hard for me.

"And do you know, Grandpa, I feel so good now, so light and easy, as if I had never been ill. The Lord Whom I just saw must have healed me! Oh, what a blessed and joyful moment it was to see my nation repenting before the face of Jehovah! I should love to see the vision again. I believe our blessed Savior will come soon to gather His people out of every land, nation, tribe, and tongue. Probably He showed me the majestic temple that will be erected in Jerusalem in the near future!"

Her friend listened quietly to her talk. This sudden change in Judith, who had been battling against death for the last days, puzzled him greatly. She had been telling of her experience, speaking in her normal, healthy voice, and her eyes were looking merrily at him. Pulse and temperature were normal, too. After a short silence, he spoke to her: "Yes, Judith, the Lord is coming soon for the world and for Israel, but for you He has come in this very hour, as I see. He has touched your sick body and has healed you. Praise and glory be to God! Let us thank Him for His loving-kindness and mercy and for His marvelous help!"

With this, the servant of Christ knelt down near the bed and poured out his heart in prayer and praise for the wonderful help and love of God.

"I can soon start to work again, can I not?" asked the patient after her fellow-laborer arose from his knees.

"Certainly. As soon as the Lord restores your strength again, you may use it anew for the glory of the Master. We shall be glad to work together again. But for the present, I consider it would be best if He would give you a good, sound sleep. We must stop talking now, and you be a good girl and try to sleep."

From this moment, Judith improved rapidly. Evidently the Lord wanted to leave His handmaiden yet for a little while here on earth. Her time had not yet come to go home to be with Him forever. There was still something for her to do here that the Lord might be glorified through her. A number of souls were waiting to be led to Christ through her ministry. The Lord manifested His love and power by restoring the health of His child, for there had been very little hope for recovery during the first period of her illness.

The time prior to her sickness had been extremely strenuous for her as well as for her co-workers with uninterrupted work and the walking of long distances from one village to the other, sometimes from twenty to thirty miles, at times without food the whole day, and not seldom under pouring rain; at other times in the burning heat of the summer sun. Besides, each had to carry a load on his back — Bibles and other books, the needed clothes and underwear, and other

Dedicated to the Lord

things of necessity. The food was very poor and scant at that time. And with this all were the persecutions of the enemies of the gospel of Jesus Christ, who invented all kinds of evil to harm the missionaries. Wherever and whenever they could, they molested and troubled them, frequently arresting them unlawfully. Sometimes whole groups of such infuriated antagonists came to the meeting ready to tear the witnesses of the truth into pieces as wolves tear the sheep. They would have done it if God had not intervened in His own marvelous way.

Shortly before Judith broke down, she had been visiting homes. She came to a house near the end of the village where she found several children desperately ill. Both parents had died of the same disease. The children were all unconscious. They were lying on the clay floor on a heap of filthy straw in one corner of the room. They had no clothes on their bodies, but were covered with a few dirty, half rotten rags. Vermin covered everything. There was nobody to look after them, and they were left to die slowly but surely.

To pass these poor, unfortunate children was impossible for Judith and her fellow-workers. Although Judith had not been feeling well lately, she, together with the others, started at once to rescue these young lives from death, if possible. After long, hard, and unpleasant work of scrubbing, washing, and cleaning, the sick found themselves on clean beds in clean and aired rooms, clothed in plain but clean gowns. A few days of proper and loving care made the patients feel a great deal better, and they were well on the way to recovery. But Judith, being tired and worn out, had contracted typhus from her patients, and she broke down under the power of the disease. For weeks she was confined to her bed, hovering between life and death. However, the loving heavenly Father came to help His true and faithful child.

During all the time of strenuous labor and in the period of her illness, Judith never forgot her dearly beloved parents and her nation. She had never heard from them again since the night her father had cast her out. All her letters had remained unanswered. This was the hardest test for her faith. Frequently she separated herself and sought a quiet place where she shed many a burning tear and where she pleaded with God for the salvation of her parents and sisters. At times the burden became almost unbearable for her that her precious mother had sent her away with such an awful curse on her lips. The thought that her mother might suddenly die without peace with God and not being reconciled to her was a great torture for Judith. She could hardly think that her beloved mother might pass into eternal peril. At such moments she felt an almost irresistible desire to go home and to entreat her mother to be reconciled to God through the Lord Jesus Christ. But the impossibility of it compelled her to give it up. Being unable to do anything for the salvation of her father, mother, and sisters herself, she fled more frequently and more earnestly to the Lord in prayer on their behalf.

Now the sickness had passed that had taken Judith away from the work for quite a number of weeks. As soon as she felt able, she threw herself fully into the blessed service to spread the gospel among those who did not know the blessed happiness of a holy life in communion with the Lord Jesus Christ.

Dedicated to the Lord

A page torn out of her diary and found accidentally after her homegoing tells us a little of this time:

"Monday, September 1st, 1919. B——. Praise be to God that He has restored my strength to me again and I am able to do at least something for my Lord! On Friday we were in the village G——, on Saturday in H——. On Sunday morning we worshiped with the Russian brethren. In the afternoon we were in the German church. Afterwards again in the Russian meeting. Later we had our joint women's gathering. After that we went to the evening service. We sang much, witnessed for our Lord, and prayed with the people. The heavenly Father glorified Himself and blessed us abundantly."

Judith was frequently asked by the peasants who gathered around her or by the sick of whom she took care and who heard her sincere simple testimony for Jesus, "How is it that you, a Jewess, preach the Lord Jesus Christ to us? For the Jews were the ones who crucified Christ, and they do not acknowledge Him even until this day."

Usually Judith told such inquirers in her meek and sweet, simple way how she found her Savior and how she dedicated her whole life to Him for service, because her only desire was to live exclusively for Him.

"But you are so young yet, and so delicate and sweet," remarked an old woman on one occasion as she interrupted Judith, who was speaking to them of the Friend of sinners Who had given His life to save us. This woman had been listening very attentively, and tears were flowing down her wrinkled cheeks.

"For us old folks it's about time to think of God, but you are so young. Here I am sitting and looking at you all the time — you are such a beautiful girl — and I cannot help but think that you are so unlike other people!"

"Why, dear Grandmother, am I not like others?" was Judith's question as she looked at the good old woman with happy, twinkling eyes.

"Why, my dear? Well others at your age do not even think of God. They all are having good times and are seeking nice sweethearts for themselves. And you — you go with your knapsack on your slender shoulders from place to place telling us of our Lord God, curing the sick and helping the poor. And you do not even take any pay for your work from any one. Oh, if only our merciful God would send to us unlearned, poor people more such good, virtuous benefactors as you!"

Judith listened to the words that came from the depth of the sincere heart of this simple woman, and she could not keep back the tears of compassion.

"Yes, Grandmother, dear," she said after a short pause; "I too was like all the others some time ago. I had all I needed for my life in abundance. I liked to have good times, too. I was engaged to a good, handsome, and rich young man. I loved pleasures and amused myself like others. Then one day I heard of my Lord and Savior, and I gave up my former sinful life, also my sweetheart, and became a bride of the Lord Jesus Christ. I have given Him my heart and my whole life. He has taught me to love everybody and to do the kind of work I am trying to do in your midst. As for my labor, He Himself will give me a wonderful reward there, in heaven, when I am going to be with Him forever. Here on earth, too. He has done much for me, and for you, too. He gave His precious life for you. He died the most cruel, painful death on the cross. His great love for us poor wretched sinners made Him do it. From us He is asking nothing except our wicked, stubborn, sin-sick heart, which He desires to wash and to cleanse with His precious

Dedicated to the Lord

blood. If we let Him do this, He will take us after death into His marvelous and glorious heavenly kingdom."

"Oh, my precious child, how I do wish to be with Him in His kingdom! I have been thinking of it much lately but I know too well that I am a great and wicked sinner before Him. How could He take such an one as me into heaven, where there are only sinless and holy people? I was once young and pretty as you, but that has passed. Now my face is covered with these ugly wrinkles. My conscience is troubling me. It is speaking loudly of my past sins, for my life in my youth was not like yours. I never thought of God, neither of death, nor of the fact that I ever would have to give an account of my sinful life before the righteous Judge. It seemed to me that I would be always young, handsome, healthy, and, now I am an old ruin. Soon my end will be here. But what then? My whole life has passed without God. My heart is stained and black with sin. All is now behind me. I can take nothing with me on that long journey that is before me. Only my sins and my shame will follow me. The thought of what awaits me on the other side of the grave frightens me. I spend many a sleepless night pondering over this question. If only the gracious God will be merciful to me, a great sinner, and will forgive my transgressions!"

Big tears of unfeigned repentance rolled down her thin, yellow, wrinkled cheeks.

Some hours later there stood a changed, happy old woman at the door of her cottage, kissing Judith heartily good-by. Her eyes were illuminated with joy and peace, as she was wishing God's rich blessing upon Judith. Through Judith, she had heard for the first time in her life of the love and saving power of Jesus Christ, and she had responded to His love and had given Him her dark, sinful heart, which He cleansed and purified with His atoning blood. And peace, wonderful peace and joy, reigned in her heart during the last days of her earthly life.

"The good Lord has sent you to me as His messenger, His angel. The loving and compassionate Shepherd has searched for me His poor, lost sheep," said the woman in her great joy. "You are going now to other distressed, sin-sick people as was I. Go, then — go, my dear — go, you bride of Christ! He Himself be with you wherever you go. I cannot go to serve Him in such a way, for my feet have become too tired from walking here on earth. I am ready now to enter joyfully into His blessed Kingdom! Death does not frighten me any longer. On the contrary, I am longing and waiting for it."

A new stream of tears ran down her cheeks. She was happy that she was saved, and on the other hand she was sorry to part with Judith.

"Good-by, dear Grandmother, now my dear sister in Christ. I have to go now. There are still many souls whom the Savior wants to draw to Himself. Perhaps we shall soon see each other there!" Judith had lifted up her face radiant with joy and was pointing upward. "The Lord be with you, dear sister, in these last days."

Putting her knapsack on her shoulders, Judith looked for the last time into the face of her new-found friend and went away.

Thus were Judith's days spent in service. The love of God and the numerous conversions that changed the lives so visibly, inspired Judith always anew. Her labor was not in vain nor fruitless.

It often happened that she was met at first coldly, often even with enmity, but her sincerity, simplicity, and her unfeigned love always won the victory over those, and not a small number of them were led by her to Calvary, where they prostrated themselves in sincere repentance and found peace, joy, and life eternal.

Those cases were a special source of joy to Judith, and it encouraged her greatly when she saw those who had manifested such hostility and hatred at first, come to Christ Jesus and humbly bow before Him, for this kindled the hope in her heart that perchance her parents, too, would in time be overcome by the love of Christ, and they, too, would bow their knees before Him Whom they now hated, their Messiah and Savior.

The trying time of Judith's severe illness had not passed without leaving a permanent impression upon her life. She arose from her bed a changed person. Having always been lively and full of joy, she was now as if transfigured. It seemed as if she had been at the Mount of Transfiguration, where the glory of the Lord had appeared to her and was reflecting upon her whole life. She had become more quiet, and a strange shadow of pensiveness was now frequently upon her countenance, which was formerly always sparkling with happy merriment. This was not sadness nor a longing for anything earthly, as for her parents or friends. She was meditating much about heavenly things after her sickness. Her whole being seemed to express a great longing for the heavenly mansions. Her soul was thirsting and longing to be with Him there. Her words and her actions were deeper and more serious than before.

This change could not escape the eyes of her fellow-workers, with whom she was in daily contact. Her most beloved subjects to talk about when walking long distances between the villages and cities were the coming of the Lord, the rapture of the church, and the meeting with Him.

"Do you know, Grandpa," she said on one of these journeys to the leader of the group of missionaries, "I have seen the Lord Jesus Christ often during my illness in different forms and in various places. But it was always in connection with His second coming. I do not know, but it seems to me more and more that He will come soon for His Church. At times I think that we must hear His voice calling at any moment.

"An inner voice, which has so many times in my life comforted, inspired, and cheered me in all circumstances of my life after my conversion, especially in times of persecution and trial, keeps telling me to be ready to meet my Lord. I am waiting for Him to come every hour. This world seemed formerly so dear to me, and I was so much concerned about earthly things, but lately the earthly things are distant and strange to me. The last days I have not even felt such a burden and grief when thinking of my dear parents. I have been able to think of them calmly. Are you feeling the same way?"

"No, Judith," was the reply of the evangelist. "I do not feel exactly as you do, but I, too, do believe that the coming of our Lord is very near. I believe that while I am still living here on earth He will appear, and I shall see Him face to face. The great desire of my heart is to live and to tell the people of His soon return. Watching you, I have noticed a great change in you since your illness. Sometimes I have been thinking that you have not fully recovered yet and that you have started out too early. The many privations and hardships are more than your frail body can stand. At times the thought comes to me to send you to one of our Christian friends for rest and recuperation. I was thinking of it even today while we were walking. You are quite tired and worn out."

"Oh, no, brother, I feel well and healthy, and the hardships in our way seem to me much easier than before I was sick. I am not thinking of rest at all. I should be most unhappy if you would send me away from the work even for a short time. The thoughts and feelings of which I told you are not the result of illness or fatigue, but exclusively from the conviction that the Lord will soon take me to Himself."

Judith spoke the last words hardly audibly and her face, shining with joy and anticipation, was lifted up, and her thoughtful eyes were looking to heaven whence she awaited her Lord and heavenly Bridegroom.

"If so, Judith, then may the Lord grant that you be ready every minute to meet Him. He is holding our time in His own hands. Perhaps the hour of your home-going is indeed very near. Or it might be that for us and for all His saints here on earth the hour of the Rapture is at hand. I am quite sure that His coming is not very far off, though I do not feel just as you do about it. Let us, therefore, work faithfully in these, probably last days, that when He comes He may find us not idle but busily engaged in the work He has foreordained for us. If ever His voice has called His own to watchfulness and labor, it surely is in our days.

"We see how the night of darkness and sin covers the nations more each day. Lawlessness is increasing rapidly and is overflowing the earth like a flood. Love is waxing cold in the hearts of many Christians. God's people in Russia are being oppressed and persecuted by the government. They have to undergo hunger, privation, and martyrdom for their faith in the Lord Jesus Christ. In western Europe, and especially in America, the Lord Jesus is being rejected and denied more alarmingly each day, and that voluntarily without any pressure or persecution.

"The lights of the church are growing dim everywhere. Misery and distress are growing and spreading all over the world like threatening monsters. God sends them as the last means to awaken the world and to warn His people that His appearance is at hand, and that the last great judgment over the world is approaching. The world is rejecting and despising God, the Lord Jesus Christ, and His laws and orders of life, increasingly. And because men do not want Him to reign over them, God permits the forerunners of Antichrist to rule. Being tired of and discontented with the commandments of life given by God, the world gets disorder and destruction.

"But one thing gladdens and comforts my heart in these days, that in these dark hours of judgment over our country, so many souls are awakening out of the sleep of sin and death and are becoming alive to God, giving their hearts and lives to Him, so that these awful shocks are not shaking our land in vain."

VI

THE YOUTHFUL MARTYR

The Clouds Grow Darker — Last Days — Faithful unto Death

IT WAS LATE in the fall. The yellow and brown leaves that were torn from the trees by the wind covered the wet ground like a colored carpet. The cold rain was pouring down in torrents.

A group of people was making its way through the woods near a village, carefully avoiding the puddles of water and mud by stepping onto the dry leaves and branches on the ground. They were thoroughly drenched from the falling rain and their clothes were muddy up to their knees. The knapsacks they carried on their shoulders with their clothes and other necessities were wet and heavy.

Approaching the village, the strangers stopped for a minute and looked around as if searching for something. Then they turned and went toward one of the little pleasant houses into which they entered after knocking at the door. The farmer and his wife greeted their guests heartily and then aided them quickly to free themselves from the wet, sticky clothing and shoes. The travelers were tired from their long walk and hungry, too, but their faces were illuminated with inner joy, and even their voices did not betray any dejection or murmuring. While they were cleaning up as much as possible, they told their hospitable hosts of their walk of about ten to twelve miles along the muddy road under pouring rain. Then they united in prayer as they knelt down, praising God for strength and protection on the way and for the happy meeting with these children of His under whose roof they had found temporary shelter.

"We are glad and really thankful to the Lord that you came this way and that you have arrived safely," said the farmer. "We and a few others here in our village have been waiting impatiently for you the last days. We were told that a little company of missionaries held the way in our direction. So we thought we would take our horses and wagon and meet you on the road. But to our grief, the rain continued, and it even grew worse so that the roads are entirely impassable. Yesterday there were troops passing our village, and they had four horses harnessed to one wagon loaded with sick and wounded soldiers, and these were hardly able to pull the vehicle through the streets. With two horses, it would be impossible to drive even a mile, especially such poor creatures as the soldiers have given me in exchange for my four good strong horses. So you will have to take the good will for the deed. Well, praise God, you are here! The Lord did not leave you without His help.

"I suppose you would like to start your mission here in our place tonight, wouldn't you? If so, I can quickly let our villagers know about it. Everyone here is so discouraged and weary from the experiences of late that even those who were greatly opposed to the gospel begin now to seek God. Our whole vicinity is occupied by armies, and most of the homes are filled with sick and wounded. The soldiers have spread typhus widely

The Youthful Martyr 145

and other diseases among the peaceful population, and there is much suffering and distress on every hand. Those who do not know God are on the verge of despair, and we are just a handful of Christians, only a few families, and even we are at times disheartened and quivering with fear, not knowing what the outcome of all this will be. Soldiers are passing through every day, plundering, threatening, and even killing. They take our last bread, cattle, clothing, and all that they fancy. To protest or hide things is impossible, for the moment they find anything hidden they shoot the owner on the spot. Yes, we are living in hard times! Who knows how it will end and what the future is going to bring us?" He finished with a heavy sigh.

"Shouldn't I start right away to go and see some of the sick people here, Grandpa?" asked one of the visitors.

"No, Judith, we all are very tired, and I reckon you not less than the rest of us. Besides, it seems to me that our good hostess is busying herself in the kitchen, preparing something for us to eat, and I suppose it will be a good thing to strengthen ourselves a little, for we are quite hungry. First of all, we must try to dry our clothing and shoes as far as it is possible. In the evening we shall have our first meeting, so we will get a little acquainted with the folk here. Tomorrow, if the Lord tarries, we shall be ready for any service He has in store for us. Evidently this place will keep us busy."

There was more work in that village and its surroundings than one small group of willing workers could accomplish. All around were hostile armies fighting each other and spreading death and destruction. Epidemic diseases, among which typhoid fever and typhus were prevailing, took even more lives of the population as well as of the soldiers than the battles.

Judith was walking like a good Samaritan in the midst of sorrow and woe in this valley of death. Cold, mud, or rain could not hinder her in her labor of love among these unfortunate people, sick in body and soul. Lending a helping hand wherever help was needed most, and taking care of the sick, she never missed an opportunity to tell them of the Lord Jesus Christ and His love to men.

When she was reading the Bible in the homes where friends and neighbors had gathered to hear her, there were often soldiers among the hearers. Some of them, touched by the Word and Spirit of God, acknowledged their sins and confessed their crimes. Not a few of these soldiers came to the feet of Christ, pleading for forgiveness, and being born again, they left their bloody way leading into eternal punishment and death and started a new, holy life following the Lord Jesus on the way leading to joy and life eternal.

The repentance of their comrades and the proclaimed truth brought others into a mad fury. They came to the meetings, where they began to contradict, to swear, and to blaspheme God and curse those who read the Bible and preached the truth.

"You are going around everywhere for the one purpose of fooling and deceiving the people with your gospel," said one of these opponents on one occasion. "We know you preachers too well! It's high time to chop off your heads, and it surely will happen on one of these days! Where were you before? I would like to know. Why didn't you speak to the capitalists of repentance when they were oppressing the poor working people? Why didn't you tell them to repent and stop exploiting the poor? Now, since we have rebelled against them and are lifting up our guns at them, you have appeared in our midst, scaring us with the tortures of hell, telling us of our sin and of the love of your Christ, exhorting us to love one another. This here is our love for you!" he shouted, brandishing his sword threateningly. "Look here, this is the best expression of our love for you and all such as you!

"Your face testifies that the sun has never burned it in the fields," continued the enraged soldier. "Neither have you ever had to breathe the heavy, biting, dusty air of the factories. But most likely you have been sitting all your life in a comfortable, wealthy nest. And now since we have destroyed these cozy nests, the birds have flown out in all directions to invoke us to love and pity you. We shall show you and your Christ our love yet!" Gnashing his teeth, he turned around and looked at the audience.

"Are there still idiots who want to listen to her reading of her gospels? This silly book of fables, hoax, and fictions. And they are even crying like old crazy women!

"Just look at her face!" — pointing with his shining sword close to Judith's face — "she is not even a Russian! Most likely she is a Jewess. Ha! Ha! She is reading to you from her story book that the Jews have crucified Christ, and she, a Jewess, is preaching this same Christ to you, representing him as God. Isn't that fun? It's enough now! She must be driven out of here. No, best of all, and the most fun would be to hang her!"

The man was laughing wildly, a hoarse devilish laughter that chilled the very soul.

As long as the Communistic soldier was speaking, Judith said nothing. She stood there with the open Bible in her hands, looking with love and compassion at her audience.

"Our friend has said several things about me that are true," Judith began, after the Communist became quiet. "He told you that I am a Jewess, and that I have never worked either in the fields or in the factories, but have lived in a comfortable home and in wealth. This is all true. He has not been mistaken in this. However, he was mistaken in his other statements. Neither the loss of my riches nor the desire to deceive my fellow-men made me leave my home. The one and only reason why I am here is the love to my Savior, the Lord Jesus Christ, and for lost souls.

"Since my early childhood I was taught the same things our friend spoke of a moment ago, namely, that the Lord Jesus Christ was a deceiver and the Gospels a collection of fables and lies. I believed what I was told and lived as all other people around me did. But, praise and glory to my Redeemer, He gave me a chance to attend a meeting similar to this one. There the Word of God was read and expounded. And there I became convinced that Jesus Christ is not a deceiver — but the Son of God, the Creator of heaven and earth, and of us, too. When the time was fulfilled He came down to our earth, and here He died for us to deliver us from sin and death and to reconcile us with God and each other.

"Sin has divided people into poor and rich, into Russians, Germans, English, Chinese, Jews, and so on.

As a result of sin, people are at enmity; they are persecuting and killing each other. They are making horrible bloody wars and brother is fighting against brother in most terrible revolutions that demolish and destroy everything good and noble. But Christ has come to unite all people into one nation, into one flock. After I learned this truth from the gospel, I ceased to count myself a Jewess. I found there that all men must be brothers and sisters and that we must love one another, for this is the will of the Lord Jesus Christ for us.

"Since the day of my conversion to Christ I was determined to go and tell this wonderful glad news of God's love to everybody everywhere. This I am telling here today to you who have gathered in this house. Why are the people hating and killing each other? Isn't he that kills just as well a human being as his victim? Is not an untimely, violent death just as terrifying to him as to those whom he murders? Are not the parents, wives, and children bewailing the death of their dear ones? I see here a number of heavily armed young men. Are not your old mothers going to shed bitter tears should they hear of your untimely death? Perhaps some of you have left at home your darling babies. Would not their suffering be great should they become orphans? And for your own self, do you want to die? And yet you are daily in constant danger of being killed by such armed men as yourselves.

"However, this is not the most important nor the most horrible thing. The most weighty question is, what awaits all of you yonder on the other side of the grave? All of us without exception have to die some day. As our lives have been here on earth, so will they be in eternity. Death separates our soul from the body, but it does not free us from our sins nor from the consequence of our sinful life, from eternal punishment. Our conscience will not be cleansed by passing through the gates of death. On the contrary, all our thoughts, words, and deeds will be manifested and revealed after our passing away from this earth. Oh, what horror and suffering to see ourselves there as we really are in the proper light of eternity. Where shall we find a hiding-place then? We cannot escape from ourselves, neither from our deeds which are following us.

"The Lord is calling you, therefore, now while it is yet the acceptable time. It is not too late yet. He is willing to wash each sin-stained heart that comes to Him, with His precious blood. He washed mine when I came to Him the first time in my life. And He will cleanse yours too, today, this very hour, if you only are willing and come to Him. Will you not accept His love and come in repenting spirit and open your hearts before Him? Will you come?"

Many tears of repentance were flowing and many a heart bowed humbly before the Lord while hearing Judith's simple testimony. It came from the depth of her heart and went straight to the hearts of others. But Satan was not idle. He stirred up his servants. The man who had threatened before became more and more infuriated as she went on. His terrible threatening look seemed to pierce Judith while he knocked nervously with his sword on the floor. At her last inviting words, he suddenly ran out of the cottage, slamming the door with a terrible oath. Throwing one more venomous look at Judith, he cried with an oath: "You will be the first one to repent of your words!"

Day after day passed by. The weather had been of late unpleasant. It was cool and rainy, and heavy storms had accompanied the rain. Everything in nature was dreary and dull, as if the shroud of death had been spread over all. But Judith seemed not to notice the gloomy picture of autumn. She was too absorbed in her duties among the afflicted and sick and in her eagerness to bring immortal souls who hunger and thirst for peace and rest to Christ. To her everything seemed bright and good, for it all seemed to be illuminated with a certain light. By day and by night she was seen walking through the street on her errands of love, no matter how dark, cold, or muddy it was. And wherever she came, she reflected the light of heaven and spread peace and joy in the valley of sin and death.

She did not notice that thick, dark, ominous clouds were gathering over her life, becoming more threatening each day. Her love for the unsaved and her expectant waiting for the coming of the Lord, hid these things from her. Nevertheless the clouds became denser and darker with every passing hour. Satan, the prince of darkness and all evil here on earth, could not sleep and be carelessly looking on the untiring labor of this faithful child of God and one soul after another being rescued from the captivity of his dark power and brought into the light and liberty of the sons of God.

Lately the devil was arming more and more cruel and wicked men against her. The hearts of these were hardened through their life of sin and crime. These dark souls hated the light Judith spread wherever she went. Their hatred grew steadily until they were ready to commit another atrocious crime.

At one of their secret conferences, they passed the resolution to kill those who constantly reminded them of their sins and of the coming judgment of God. They were determined to remove the light from their dark path leading into hell for eternity. A few days later their devilish plan was realized.

At daybreak one of the gloomy, foggy mornings of the fall, there was a lonely man making his way carefully over the fields sowed with winter wheat. He was evidently coming from one village and was heading for another. Every few minutes he was looking timidly around in every direction as if fearing something. There had been a hard frost at night and that enabled him to walk over the loose, plowed ground. The lonely wanderer was very anxious to keep away as far as possible from the roads and was evidently hiding from someone or at least he tried to conceal the direction of his journey.

A deep, unutterable grief was plainly written on his countenance. Heavy sighs escaped his pressed breast, and he lifted his distressed eyes in anguish up to heaven. Now he had reached the last little hill and was slowly descending into the valley before him in which the village of Andrejevka was spread out. The whole valley was wrapped in a heavy fog.

The wanderer stopped for a moment or two. Looking carefully around, he turned finally to the left and started to make his way through the neglected orchards and gardens behind the houses. Now and then he heard human voices or the cry of domestic fowls and cattle waking up from their sleep.

When he almost reached the other end of the village, he walked hesitatingly toward an old abandoned barn that was a little distance from the other farm buildings. It had been used formerly as a storage place for hay and other fodder for the cattle but was now empty and abandoned. Coming near, the stranger halted once more and looked carefully around. Then he approached slowly, as if dreading to go in at the large door of the barn. His face had turned deathly white, and his pale lips were painfully pressed together, and his whole body was shaking. With trembling hands, he opened the heavy door that shrieked loudly on its rusty hinges. He entered and closed the door tightly. Making a few steps into the interior, he stopped abruptly before a dark object on the ground. In the darkness he could not see what it was.

Going back, he opened the door slightly to let some light in. Turning, he saw a ghastly picture before him that made the blood run cold in his veins. About a yard or two from the door there was the lifeless form of a young girl mutilated by cruel swords. It was evident that the young martyr had been on her knees praying when she breathed her last breath. Her left hand, now cold and lifeless, was still holding the Bible she had pressed to her breast in the last moments here on earth. The Book was saturated with her blood. Her right hand was under the cut and mutilated head.

For a few silent, solemn minutes he looked at the earthly remains from which the soul had escaped to go home. A deep groan lifted his sore breast.

"Poor Judith!" he said softly. "Here you have found the end of your life in this world . . . Well, you are happy now, for you are now with Him to Whom your heart belonged, for Whom you lived and labored here, and for whose sake you have died a martyr's death. Who knows, perhaps my end will come soon, too. . . . It may be that Grandpa will soon follow you.

"It is too great a risk to stand here any longer!" he said to himself after a moment of pathetic quietness. "Her murderers are still in the village and should one of them espy me here they would quickly put an end to my life, too. Perhaps it is not time for me yet? There is so much work to be done everywhere." After another painful look at the blood-covered body before him, he said regretfully, "We have not even a chance to bury her earthly tabernacle!"

With a long last look at the remains of Judith, he left, heart-broken, the scene of this atrocious murder and, retracing his steps through the orchards, he was able to reach the other village unnoticed.

Judith had gone home. She had died blessing and praying for her murderers. The day before her home-going, after having prayer-fellowship for the last time together, Judith bade Grandpa and the other missionaries good-by and went to the neighboring village. There she started the work in her usual way by visiting the homes and witnessing for her Lord in word and deed. About four o'clock, a large number of the villagers gathered in one of the homes to listen to her as she read and explained the old, and yet always new gospel of salvation.

She was speaking of her Savior that day with great enthusiasm and love. The Lord seemed to be nearer to her than ever before. It was as if she could almost see Him with her physical eyes in the midst of the assembled people. All present listened with tense interest and devotion.

Suddenly there was a wild noise, and in came a number of heavily armed soldiers. It was evident that they had come for an evil purpose. Judging from their behavior, they had come to carry out their satanic resolution which they had made recently.

"Get out of here, everyone to his home if you desire to live any longer!" was the severe command of one of the men.

"We need only her — over there," he added after a minute, pointing with his saber to Judith.

Another drew out his sword, which reflected the rays of the afternoon sun, and went up to the girl, who stood calmly behind the table with the open Bible in her hand.

The assembled people left the place, which would in a moment be a new scene of bloodshed, as hurriedly as they could, each running to his home in a panic. They had seen many massacres and they knew by this time this type of people could be stopped by nobody and nothing. These wicked men were used to carrying out their evil purposes regardless of anything. Before long Judith was alone in the midst of these devil-possessed men.

"Who are you?" asked the man close by her side brutally. "Who has sent you to spread this opium among the people? Who has bribed you to persuade our soldiers in our armies to love their neighbors and even their enemies in a time when they must mercilessly kill and destroy all such 'white hands' and lazy folks as yourself? Answer immediately! This is the last hearing we are giving you!"

Judith stood quietly, looking with deep, heartfelt compassion upon these wicked men before her. After a minute's pause, she replied: "Who I am there is no need to tell you, for you knew it long since. Anyway, I can tell you once more that I am a Jewess converted to the Lord Jesus Christ, being now His disciple and follower. He it is who has sent me to all people and to you, too, to tell you that He has died for you, that He loves you and wants to save you. He is inviting you this very hour once more to leave your sinful life and turn to Him with all your heart.

"He has purchased me, giving Himself as a sacrifice for me. He has paid the high price of His own blood on the cross of Calvary for my redemption. He has done the same for you. He loves you with an undefiled, pure and holy love, and He has sent me to tell you of it today."

"Sinko, give orders to your saber to stop that ever babbling tongue forever! We are sick of such speeches! It's enough," was the savage command of the officer.

"Stop! No; she isn't worthy that we dirty the floor of this cottage with her blood. Lead her into a barn or any such place!"

"Follow me!" roared the soldier who had questioned her with a hoarse voice, turning to leave the house. The others, lifting up their swords, encircled Judith. They were leading her thus to an abandoned barn in the rear of an orchard.

Judith realized only too well that the last moment of her earthly life had come. In an instant, she would be united with her Savior and Lord forever. Walking in the midst of these brutal men, she knew no fear. She was using the last precious minutes of her life to tell them of the love of the Lord Jesus Christ to them and of the necessity to repent and give their hearts to Him.

Upon entering the barn, she fell on her knees, and for the last time here on earth she turned to God in supplication and prayer for her beloved parents.

"I am coming to Thee, my Savior and my Lord. But Thou knowest that I am leaving here on earth those whom I love unspeakably. I pray Thee, my God, don't let them perish in the iniquity of their hearts. Save them, O Lord, and draw them nigh unto Thee. Please forgive my dear mother for treating me unjustly. Let not this sin be upon her, my God!"

An unseen hand stayed the hands of the wicked men until Judith finished her last petition to God. They were as if paralyzed and looked without saying a word at the girl kneeling in their midst. The unseen power kept them, not permitting them to dishonor or defile the faithful handmaiden of Christ.

"Forgive, O Lord, these poor men who are about to end my life here in this world. Do not lay this sin upon them, but let Thy pierced hand touch their hearts that they may come to Thee! Do forgive them, my God, and do not ask my blood from their hands — for they do not know what they are doing!"

As she was uttering the last words the shining blades of the sabers brandished over her head and, whistling through the air, came down, cutting deep gashes through her dark curly hair, into her head. The last words died on Judith's pale lips as a stream of crimson blood gushed out of her head and body, staining the clothes of the devil-inspired men.

Exchanging silent glances, the murderers turned around and left the gruesome scene in the barn. The meek quietness and the undisturbed peace of Judith, and her last prayer, had astounded these cruel, hardened hearts and had closed their lips. Their deadened conscience began to speak once more. Staring at the ground, they left without dropping a word.

During the night the tragic news of Judith's death reached the missionaries in the next village. And very early before the dusk of the night disappeared, Grandpa started out to see if the rumors were really true. He managed to enter the village and find Judith's mutilated body without being seen by the soldiers. Not being able to bury her remains, he asked some of the peasants to put the body into the grave for its last rest.

Not one of her friends, relatives, or acquaintances was present as the men took Judith's lifeless body to bury it in the cemetery, but He for Whom she had lived and died was there, and He spoke through her death to these simple, good-hearted peasants.

"How she did love the people!" remarked one of the peasants, wiping the tears from his sun-burned, bearded cheeks as they lowered the body without a casket into the grave. "How much good she has done in our vicinity, taking care of the sick and comforting and helping those who needed help. And she did it all without ever expecting thanks from the people and never did she take any remuneration for her labor. She always used to answer, 'My Savior, the Lord Jesus Christ has paid me already for it.' It was evident that she loved God with her whole heart. She was a Jewess — but how she did venerate and love the Lord Jesus, and how fervent were her prayers to Him!"

"Yes, as she taught, so she lived! By her, word and deed were not contrary, they were in full harmony," added another.

"And here is the book from which she always read so many good things. She has been holding it even in death in her lifeless hand. And look — it's all covered with her own blood. The way she was holding it shows that it was very dear to her. She died on her knees, praying until the last moment."

The peasant took the edge of his short, warm coat and wiped the big tears away that rolled down his face into the heavy beard.

"Perhaps we should put the book with her into the grave?" asked one of them, as he took a shovel to cover Judith's body.

"Yes, that's right," agreed the others. "All the leaves inside are saturated and crimson, too. It's best to put it with her into the grave."

"The kingdom of heaven be yours, dear Miss! We did not know you, who you were nor where your parents and home are, but you loved us all, and we knew and felt it."

With this, the men began to fill the grave with earth.

"If only God in His mercy would send to us sinners more such good people!" sighed one of the men, pausing for a minute in his work.

"Why is it that there are so many bad, wicked people and so few good ones in this world? And even these few are being killed mercilessly. There are several of these people here in our neighborhood, but the poor souls cannot even dare to show themselves here while their co-worker is being buried, saying nothing that they cannot have a decent funeral for her, no

They would be killed immediately should they be seen here."

"Hush! Theodor, don't dare to say such things aloud, for who knows — walls and bushes have ears in these days. Should anyone hear us say things like that, we might inflict danger, even death upon these good folk."

Now the earth covers the cold, breathless body of Judith, until the trump of God shall sound and the dead in Christ shall rise on that glorious morning. No one will ever see her here on earth again, but her labor of love will live for a long time yet in the hearts of those who have experienced this love in their lives. Many of those who have met her here and listened to her will meet her in glory with Him Whom she so loved. Many a star will sparkle in her crown, with which her head will be adorned forever.

AUTHOR'S NOTE: The book, *Judith*, is a true narrative of the life of a girl, the daughter of a prominent Jewish family in Russia. After accepting the Lord Jesus Christ as her Saviour, Judith was compelled to leave her father's house, the young man to whom she was engaged and whom she loved dearly, her friends and her people. Her life, that henceforth was fully yielded and consecrated to the service of her Lord, found an end under the deadly blows of the swords of a group of soldiers.

It was the author's privilege to observe Judith's life and service for Christ and to witness her untimely end. The story of her life from childhood to her conversion is based upon the author's recollection of many personal discourses with Judith.

Names have been changed in this book because of existing conditions in Russia.

This narrative, published by the author in the Russian language, has brought great blessings to many in Poland, Rumania, and other countries. With the hope and prayer that it will also bring blessings to many in America, *Judith* is being sent forth now in the English language.